Questions Inmates Ask About
GOD & JESUS
with Biblical Answers

Third Edition

John E. Lamar

Gotham Books

30 N Gould St.
Ste. 20820, Sheridan, WY 82801
https://gothambooksinc.com/

Phone: 1 (307) 464-7800

© 2024 *John E. Lamar*. All rights reserved.

No part of this book may be reproduced, stored in a retrieval system, or transmitted by any means without the written permission of the author.

Published by Gotham Books (July 1, 2024)

  ISBN: 979-8-3302-5810-9 (P)
  ISBN: 979-8-3302-5811-6 (E)

Because of the dynamic nature of the Internet, any web addresses or links contained in this book may have changed since publication and may no longer be valid.

The views expressed in this work are solely those of the author and do not necessarily reflect the views of the publisher, and the publisher hereby disclaims any responsibility for them.

Dedication

This book is dedicated to all those who faithfully serve in any Jail and Prison ministry with the hope that these questions and answers may prove useful to them.

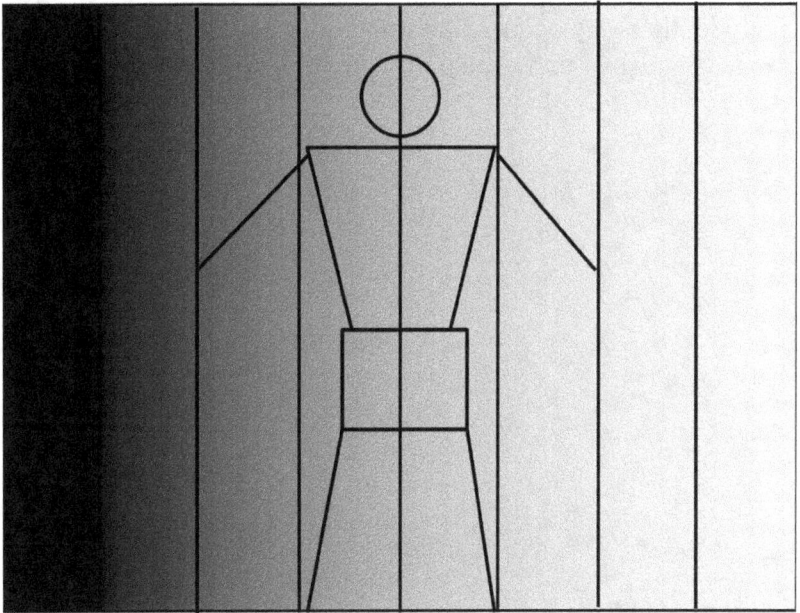

Abstract

Thinking people have questions about God and Jesus, even prison or jail inmates. This book lists questions submitted by inmates at the Newport News City Farm in Newport News, VA over a ten-year period starting in the late 1990s, along with answers by the author. The topics covered include theology, Christian walk, death, how to hear from God, baptism, and speaking in tongues, among others.

Acknowledgments

I am privileged to be able to acknowledge many of those who have contributed to the efforts that have led to this book. They are:

- My wife, Joyce, who has had to be alone on Saturday nights for the last 10+ years while I pursued ministering to the inmates at the Newport News City Farm (NNCF). I am also grateful to her for the unfailing love and support she has given me while I pursued the ministry path on which God has led me. Moreover, she has served as my English/grammar advisor, so any mistakes found in this text in those areas are due to my stubbornness and not due to her efforts.

- My colleagues from the Southeastern Correctional Ministry, Inc. (SCM) who went with me on many of those Saturday nights over the years, including Bradie Burson, Fred Hayman, Wallace Williams, Hersey Quinn and Luke Young. Their support and input has been invaluable to this ministry and in helping to address the questions posed by the inmates.

- The inmates at the NNCF who provided both the request for an opportunity to ask questions and in turn provided them.

- The SCM Senior Chaplains I have served under: Norman Rush, Sr., Jack Smith, and Gary Tingwald. These godly men have influenced me in many ways and provided assistance in terms of additional colleagues to accompany me at the NNCF.

- Pastor Bob Collins of the World Outreach Worship Center – a Church of God (Cleveland, TN) congregation in

Newport News, VA – under whose preaching/teaching I have sat for more than 30 years. Certainly, some of the answers in this book have come from his Bible teachings– either directly or indirectly.

- Pastor Hal Harter who joyfully undertook the task of reading my answers and offering many helpful suggestions.

- The *"Spirit Bade Me Go"* publisher, **Bridge-Logos, Inc.**, for permission to use portions of that book here.

- The *Holy Spirit* who has brought to my remembrance Scriptures and other references.

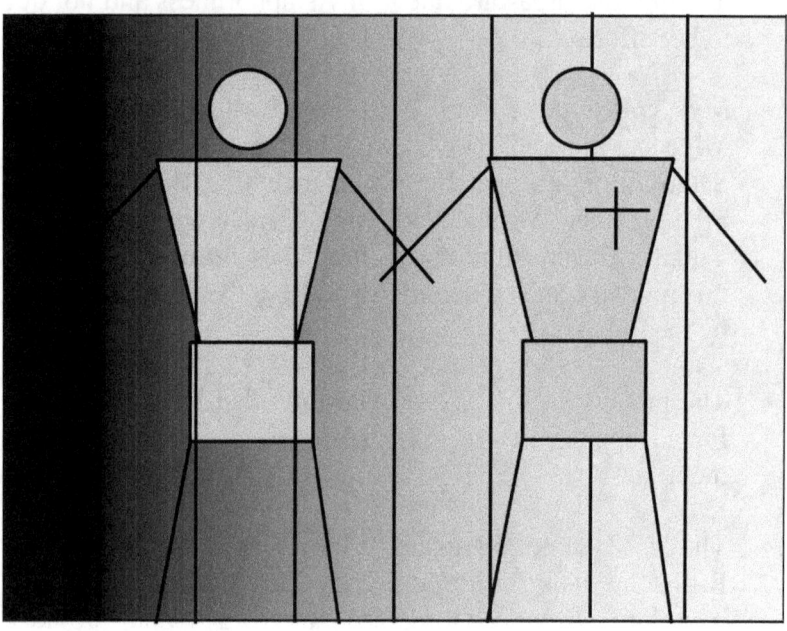

Preface

This book is not about why one does ministry in prisons or jails, because that has already been settled by Jesus in **Matthew 25:39-40**, but is dedicated to those who have already been called and have responded in loving obedience to their Lord. It is the experience of one jail chaplain and written in hope that these questions with answers may be of value to others who serve the Master in any capacity.

Since many of the questions posed by the inmates deal with issues that the Christian church has *__raised__* and *__struggled with__* over the years, it is likely that the reader will look for and find his/her favorite *doctrinal test question* in here. If you find it, then you will want to know whether my answer is in agreement with what you believe to be *sound doctrine*. I ask you to be patient with me and to view this book in its entirety without prejudging it based on my answer to your *test question*.

Abbreviations of Holy Bible translations used in the book

KJV – King James Version

NKJ – New King James Version

NIV – New International Version

NEB – New English Version

Content

Dedication iii

Abstract iv

Acknowledgments v

Preface vii

Chapter 1 – Introduction 1

Chapter 2 – Theology 3

Chapter 3 – Christian Walk 38

Chapter 4 – On Death 57

Chapter 5 – How to hear from God 66

Chapter 6 – Baptism 74

Chapter 7 – Speaking in Tongues 77

Chapter 8 – Other Topics 79

Chapter 9 – Closing thoughts 83

References 84

Appendix 86

Chapter 1 – Introduction

During the late 1990s, an inmate at the Newport News City Farm (NNCF) suggested to a group of volunteer ministers that the inmates be given an opportunity to ask questions about God, Jesus, and Christianity which had troubled them. Even though this inmate had listened to many useful Bible lessons brought to him at the NNCF by volunteers, these did not necessarily address his particular need. When the author began to be a weekly volunteer minister, and later chaplain at the NNCF, this request was remembered and inmates were afforded the opportunity.

The guidelines employed for the questions are simple; namely, they must not be too general and, when answered fully, would remove a hindrance to the spiritual growth of the inmate. The process is a simple one in which inmates suggest questions. These are then listed on a chalk board and, if there is an abundance of questions, the order of addressing them in the chapel service is voted on by the inmates. Lastly, all those in attendance, along with the Southeastern Correctional Ministry (SCM) volunteers, are to research the chosen question for the following weekly service. All answers must have a biblical basis which can be cited. Over the years, there were periods of time when the inmate population had no particular questions. During such times, prior inmate questions were re-posed and those of interest were addressed.

While at first one might take a dismissive attitude to the questions inmates may ask, I have found that there is much to learn from those living a Christian life in an exposed environment. These men have no place to hide and deal daily with others from backgrounds, Christian and non-Christian, different than your own. Some of the questions are from new believers while others are from those mature in the faith.

Moreover, some of these questions have been deep and led me to insightful discoveries. Perhaps you have already experienced the same during your own times of counseling or a similar question-and-answer session in your ministry, but it was somewhat new for me.

The questions are grouped according to specific topics, and these appear in the order of the most-to-least frequently asked; also, they form the chapter sequence employed in this book. These questions have very limited editing and basically appear in the form asked. It may be of interest to the reader to note that some questions have been repeated over the years. Even though I knew the background of the questions, I was surprised, during the compilation of this book, to note that many of the questions dealt with the general topic of theology.

I have included my own answers for completeness. Naturally, these are **biased** based on my own Christian training first as a member of the Methodist Church, which became the United Methodist Church, and now the Church of God (Cleveland, TN).

As this book was being written, it became clear that an appendix was needed for relevant, but ancillary, information associated with a few of the questions. These are marked with an *. As this information did not directly bear on the questions being answered, it is only included for those interested.

CHAPTER 2 – THEOLOGY

2.1   Why did God *let* Jesus die?

Scripture teaches in several places about the necessity for the death of Jesus in order to deal with our SIN and how it was in the *plan* of God (Father, Son and Holy Sprit) from the beginning. These include:

John 10:18 (KJV) "No man taketh it from me, but I *lay it down* of myself. I have power to *lay it down*, and I have power to take it again. This commandment have I received of my Father."

Hebrews 10:11-12 (KJV) "And every priest standeth daily ministering and offering oftentimes the same sacrifices, which can never take away sins: But this man, after he had *offered one sacrifice for sins for ever*, sat down on the right hand of God"

1 John 3:16 (KJV) "Hereby perceive we the love *of God*, because he [Jesus] laid down his *life* for us: and we ought to lay down *our* lives for the brethren." and

Revelation 13:7-8 (NIV) "… the Lamb that was slain from the creation of the world."

The death of Jesus, however, was only the *first part of the plan*; the *second part* was His resurrection. Scripture also teaches this in several places, including:

John 2:19 (KJV) "Jesus answered and said unto them, Destroy this temple, and in three days I will *raise* it up."

Acts 2:24 (KJV) "Whom God hath *raised* up, having loosed the pains of death: because it was not possible that he should be holden of it."

Romans 6:4 (KJV) "Therefore we are buried with him by baptism into death: that like as Christ was *raised* up from the dead by the glory of the Father, even so we also should walk in newness of life." and

Romans 8:11 (KJV) "But if the Spirit of him that *raised* up Jesus from the dead dwell in you, he that *raised* up Christ from the dead shall also quicken your mortal bodies by his Spirit that dwelleth in you."

So, the answer to the question is that during the life of Jesus on earth, He not only taught about the Kingdom of God, but He also authenticated His position of authority with miracles, and then became ***the sacrifice*** we all needed for our ***sin debt*** payment. This is so that we might have continual access to God, based on our repentance of sin and dead works, by reliance upon and faith in what Jesus did for us.

2.2 *Do you have to believe everything a teacher/preacher says?*

The basic answer is no, but you should respect what they tell you and then **check it out** for yourself with the Bible. That book will not lead you astray, even though some well-intentioned teachers/preachers may. Also, do not settle for the traditions of men about Christianity, but seek Biblical answers. The New Testament is very clear in terms of what to do, so just don't get confused by what you have heard or may hear from a teacher/preacher without **verifying** that what is being taught/preached conforms to Scripture. Jesus said in

Luke 21:33 (KJV) that "Heaven and earth shall pass away: but my words shall not pass away." So we can have confidence in His words but not in anything else.

2.3   Why is there a need for a second coming [of the Lord]?

The Messiah is a prophet, priest, and king, and He must come <u>twice</u> in order to fulfill all the His roles. The first time He comes is to do His *prophetic and priestly functions* as recorded in

Isaiah 53:2-10 (KJV) "For he shall grow up before him as a tender plant, and as a root out of a dry ground: he hath no form nor comeliness; and when we shall see him, there is no beauty that we should desire him. He is despised and rejected of men; a man of sorrows, and acquainted with grief: and we hid as it were our faces from him; he was despised, and we esteemed him not. Surely he hath borne our griefs, and carried our sorrows: yet we did esteem him stricken, smitten of God, and afflicted. But he was wounded for our transgressions, he was bruised for our iniquities: the chastisement of our peace was upon him; and with his stripes we are healed. All we like sheep have gone astray; we have turned every one to his own way; and the LORD hath laid on him the iniquity of us all. He was oppressed, and he was afflicted, yet he opened not his mouth: he is brought as a lamb to the slaughter, and as a sheep before her shearers is dumb, so he openeth not his mouth. He was taken from prison and from judgment: and who shall declare his generation? for he was cut off out of the land of the living: for the transgression of my people was he stricken. And he made his grave with the wicked, and with the rich in his death; because he had done no violence, neither was any deceit in his mouth. ***Yet it pleased the LORD to bruise him; he hath put him to grief: when thou shalt make his soul an***

offering for sin, he shall see his seed, he shall prolong his days, and the pleasure of the LORD shall prosper in his hand."

These events were preceded by His entrance into Jerusalem. The manner of His entrance was even important because, when a king came into a city/town on an ass, this meant he came in peace. Thus, our Messiah came in peace to Jerusalem during the last week of his earthly life to set the stage by which **He would become the sacrifice we needed and become our High Priest.**

Jesus' first entrance was in His priestly role, not recognized as King by those in Jewish authority, but His kingship was recognized by Pontius Pilate. Moreover, it was prophesized in

Zechariah 9:9 (KJV) "Rejoice greatly, O daughter of Zion; shout, O daughter of Jerusalem: behold, thy King cometh unto thee: he is just, and having salvation; lowly, and riding upon an ass, and upon a colt the foal of an ass." and fulfilled by Him in

Matthew 21:5-7 (KJV) "Tell ye the daughter of Sion, Behold, thy King cometh unto thee, meek, and sitting upon an ass, and a colt the foal of an ass. And the disciples went, and did as Jesus commanded them, And brought the ass, and the colt, and put on them their clothes, and they set him thereon."

His return, or coming back, is in two parts; first before the Great Tribulation to catch the dead and alive saints away, then to rule and reign. The first part is detailed in

1Thessalonians 4:16-18 (KJV) "For the Lord himself shall descend from heaven with a shout, with the voice of the archangel, and with the trump of God: and the dead in Christ shall rise first: Then we which are alive and remain shall be caught up together with them in the clouds, to meet the Lord in the air: and so shall we ever be with the Lord. Wherefore comfort one another with these words."

John 14:3 (KJV) "And if I go and prepare a place for you, I will come again, and receive you unto myself; that where I am, there ye may be also." and

John 14:28 (KJV) "Ye have heard how I said unto you, I go away, and come again unto you. If ye loved me, ye would rejoice, because I said, I go unto the Father: for my Father is greater than I."

The second part is included in the following Scriptures:

Acts 1:11 (KJV) "Which also said, Ye men of Galilee, why stand ye gazing up into heaven? this same Jesus, which is taken up from you into heaven, shall so come in like manner as ye have seen him go into heaven.". *But this time, He will be revealed as who He truly is, as recorded in*

Revelation 19:11-16 (KJV) "And I saw heaven opened, and behold a white horse; and he that sat upon him was called Faithful and True, and in righteousness he doth judge and make war. His eyes were as a flame of fire, and on his head were many crowns; and he had a name written, that no man knew, but he himself. And he was clothed with a vesture dipped in blood: and his name is called The Word of God. And the armies which were in heaven followed him upon white horses, clothed in fine linen, white and clean. And out of his mouth goeth a sharp sword, that with it he should smite the nations: and _he shall rule them with a rod of iron_: and he treadeth the winepress of the fierceness and wrath of Almighty God. And he hath on his vesture and on his thigh a name written, KING OF KINGS, AND LORD OF LORDS."

2.4 Out of the 70 weeks in Daniel 9:24-26, how do we get the seven years of tribulation?

First, let us look at the cited Scriptures in

Daniel 9:24-26 (NKJ) "Seventy weeks are determined for your people and for your holy city, to finish the transgression, to make an end of sins, to make reconciliation for iniquity, to bring in everlasting righteousness, to seal up vision and prophecy, and to anoint the Most Holy. Know therefore and understand, that from the going forth of the command to restore and build Jerusalem until Messiah the Prince, there shall be seven weeks and sixty-two weeks; the street shall be built again, and the wall, even in troublesome times. And after the sixty-two weeks Messiah shall be cut off, but not for Himself; and the people of the prince who is to come shall destroy the city and the sanctuary. The end of it shall be with a flood, and till the end of the war desolations are determined."

I am not an expert in prophecy, but my understanding of Daniel's weeks is that they are to be counted as years. The cited verses deal with the first coming of the Messiah and foretell the accomplishment of His mission by bringing in righteousness through His sacrificial death. From Daniel to the appearance of the Messiah is 69x7 or 483 years and the final 7 years are to follow the Church Age, which was ushered in by *John the Baptist* (See **Mark 1:1-4** & **Luke 16:16**) and *Jesus*. This age continues until the Church is taken out of the way.

Regarding the seven years of the Great Tribulation, we learn from [1] that it is "A short but intense period of distress and suffering at the end of time. The exact phrase, the great tribulation, is found only once in the Bible <**Revelation 7:14**>. The great tribulation is to be distinguished from the general tribulation a believer faces in the world <**Matthew**

13:21; John 16:33; Acts 14:22>. It is also to be distinguished from God's specific wrath upon the unbelieving world at the end of the age **<Mark 13:24; Romans 2:5-10; 2 Thessalonians 1:6>**.

The great tribulation fulfills Daniel's prophecies **<Daniel 7–12>**. It will be a time of evil from false christs and false prophets **<Mark 13:22>** when natural disasters will occur throughout the world."

2.5 *What about the Trinity; Father, Jesus [the Word of God], and the Holy Spirit?* *

2.6 *How do you know that the Trinity is real?*

This basic truth is taught in many parts of Scripture, but the most direct reference is in

I John 5:7 (NKJ) "For there are three that bear witness in heaven: the Father, the Word, and the Holy Spirit; and these three are one." These three-in-one constitute the Trinity. We are not referring to three Gods, which you would get if you simply tried to add up these three parts; instead there is only one God, or Godhead, and that is composed of three cooperating parts. It is better understood if one thinks in terms of multiplying the three parts together with each part having His own specific purpose.

An example of the Trinity working together is given by the raising of Jesus Christ from the dead as detailed in

John 2:19, 21 (KJV) "*Jesus* answered and said unto them, Destroy this temple, and in three days I will raise it up.... But he spake of the temple of his body."

Romans 6:4 (KJV) "Therefore we are buried with him by baptism into death: that like as Christ was raised up from the dead by the glory of the *Father*, even so we also should walk in newness of life."

Romans 8:11 (KJV) "But if the *Spirit* of him that raised up Jesus from the dead dwell in you, he that raised up Christ from the dead shall also quicken your mortal bodies by his Spirit that dwelleth in you." and all three (triune Godhead) are involved according to

Acts 2:24 (KJV) "Whom *God hath raised up*, having loosed the pains of death: because it was not possible that he should be holden of it."

Moreover, God has made us in His image, according to

Genesis 1:26 (NIV) "Then God said, 'Let us make man in our image, in our likeness…'" and we are a *triune* being according to

1Thessalonians 5:23 (NIV) "… May your whole *spirit, soul* and *body* be kept blameless at the coming of our Lord Jesus Christ." However, this is not the only place we experience a 'trinity'. For example, we measure **time** in terms of *past, present,* and *future*; and we know that an **object** has *length, width,* and *height*. (These examples were given in an undated broadcast sermon by *Dr. D. James Kennedy* on the **Coral Ridge Hour** from the Coral Ridge Presbyterian Church, FL.)

2.7 What is purgatory?

This is a Roman Catholic teaching and they are better able to answer the question than I am. However, I can say that it is not a part of the Protestant tradition or our understanding of Scripture; *e.g.*

Hebrews 9:27 (KJV) "And as it is appointed unto men once to die, but after this the judgment:"

2.8 Where did Jesus' spirit go during the three days before the resurrection?

Scripture teaches that Jesus went to get the keys to death, hell, and the grave; moreover, He took away the very 'fear of death', or the 'sting of death', according to:

Revelation 1:18 (NIV) "I am the Living One; I was dead, and behold I am alive for ever and ever! And I hold the keys of death and Hades." and

1 Corinthians 15:56-57 (NIV) "The sting of death is sin, and the power of sin is the law. But thanks be to God! He gives us the victory through our Lord Jesus Christ." His death was sufficient for all we needed ***to live a victorious life***.

2.9 What is the difference between iniquity and sin?

Iniquity is the pre-disposition to sin (*sin-nature*) in the soul of man that is eventually manifested in the flesh. Primarily, it denotes "not an action, but the character of an action" [2]. **Sin** on the other hand is specifically an action of "thought, word or deed", primarily against God. (See [3] for more details on avoiding both.)

2.10 What do we do to get one to accept the deception that some groups have changed the 'Word of God' for their gain?

We use the TRUTH because Jesus is the Truth. However, even with truth, some are so deceived that they don't even know they are in that condition. Truth, when repeated, will produce doubt in them, and then the deception can be broken.

We can also use training we may have had and materials in our possession to confirm the **truth** and to point out **error**.

*2.11 Have the events of the Book of Revelation all taken place?**

No, but some have. Specifically, the birth of Jesus as told in the stars in

Revelation 12:4-5 (KJV) "And his tail drew the third part of the stars of heaven, and did cast them to the earth: and the dragon stood before the woman which was ready to be delivered, for to devour her child as soon as it was born. And she brought forth a man child, who was to rule all nations with a rod of iron: and her child was caught up unto God, and to his throne." Also, the fight with God, which predated mankind on the earth as recorded in

Revelation 12:7-9 (KJV) "And there was war in heaven: Michael and his angels fought against the dragon; and the dragon fought and his angels, And prevailed not; neither was their place found any more in heaven. And the great dragon was cast out, that old serpent, called the Devil, and Satan, which deceiveth the whole world: he was cast out into the earth, and his angels were cast out with him."

Another example is the seven church ages or dispensations as recorded in the passages of **Revelation 2:1, 8, 12, 18; 3:1, 7, 14.** The preceding are things that have happened or we are in. But we are approaching the last part of the last days in which there will be a rapid accumulation of events, all happening at once. This will be more than most of us can comprehend or fathom without the help of God. The rest of the **Book of Revelation** will be happening soon!

2.12 What is so amazing about Grace?

This question is so amazing in that it is the exact title of a sermon preached by Dr. D. James Kennedy [4] which uses as a basis the Scriptural text

Ephesians 2:7-10 (KJV) "That in the ages to come he might shew the exceeding riches of his grace in his kindness toward us through Christ Jesus. For by grace are ye saved through faith; and that not of yourselves: it is the gift of God: Not of works, lest any man should boast. For we are his workmanship, created in Christ Jesus unto good works, which God hath before ordained that we should walk in them."

Without going into all the details of his sermon [4], I will summarize it by giving the main points. Firstly, _grace_ is so amazing because it is *so rare*. In this life, we hope to get what we pay for or deserve, but grace is not at all like that. In fact, it is all out of proportion to what we deserve. Secondly, _grace_ is so amazing because it is *so undeserved* and counters the consequence of our root problem, which is sin. Thirdly, _grace_ is so amazing because it is *so powerful* due to its ability to change the lives of even hardened men for God's glory. And fourthly, _grace_ is so amazing because it is *so expensive* – it cost Jesus Christ His life.

2.13 Why do the Americans use the Hispanic name Jesus [Christ] when God told the Hebrew people that His son's name is Yeshua?

The basic answer is that around 300 to 400 A.D. there was a successful attempt made by the leaders of the gentile church to _deemphasize_ the Jewishness of Jesus, and the Jewish roots of the Christian church. These leaders sought to make the church more appealing to the vast number of gentiles by ignoring the fact that the churches in the first century were overwhelmingly composed of Jewish believers in Messiah.

To complete the task, this meant changing many of the names from being Jewish/Hebrew in the New Testament to those more Greek/Roman-like. Thus, the name Yeshua was changed to Jesus, Miriam was changed to Mary, etc.

2.14   When does God give up on you?

At Hell's doorstep – No!

In Hell itself? – Unfortunately, yes.

What about those who have lived a sinful life? Remember that Noah preached to those in his day:

2 Peter 2:5-14 (KJV) "And spared not the old world, but saved Noah the eighth person, a preacher of righteousness, bringing in the flood upon the world of the ungodly; And turning the cities of Sodom and Gomorrha into ashes condemned them with an overthrow, making them an ensample unto those that after should live ungodly;

And delivered just Lot, vexed with the filthy conversation of the wicked: (For that righteous man dwelling among them, in seeing and hearing, vexed his righteous soul from day to day with their unlawful deeds;) **The Lord knoweth how to deliver the godly out of temptations, and to reserve the unjust unto the day of judgment to be punished**: But chiefly them that walk after the flesh in the lust of uncleanness, and despise government. Presumptuous are they, selfwilled, they are not afraid to speak evil of dignities.

Whereas angels, which are greater in power and might, bring not railing accusation against them before the Lord. But these, as natural brute beasts, made to be taken and destroyed, speak evil of the things that they understand not; and shall utterly perish in their own corruption; And shall receive the reward of unrighteousness, as they that count it pleasure to riot in the day time. Spots they are and blemishes, sporting themselves with their own deceiving while they feast with you; Having eyes full of adultery, and that cannot cease from sin; beguiling unstable souls: an heart they have exercised with covetous practices; cursed children:"

How far will God go? He came from *heaven to earth* to save us as described in **John 1:1-14**. Also, we find Him still active in the process from

Hebrews 7:25 (KJV) "Wherefore he is able also to save them to the uttermost that come unto God by him, seeing he ever liveth to make intercession for them."

What about the role of Jesus? His role is given in the following Scriptures:

Mark 10:45 (KJV) "For even the Son of man came not to be ministered unto, but to minister, and to give his life a ransom for many."

Luke 19:10 (KJV) "For the Son of man is come to seek and to save that which was lost."

John 17:2-3 (KJV) "As thou hast given him power over all flesh, that he should give eternal life to as many as thou hast given him. And this is life eternal, that they might know thee the only true God, and Jesus Christ, whom thou hast sent." and

Romans 6:23 (KJV) "For the wages of sin is death; but the gift of God is eternal life through Jesus Christ our Lord."

What about someone who repents on his/her deathbed?

Ezekiel 33:18-20 (KJV) "When the righteous turneth from his righteousness, and committeth iniquity, he shall even die thereby. But if the wicked turn from his wickedness, and do that which is lawful and right, he shall live thereby. Yet ye say, The way of the Lord is not equal. O ye house of Israel, I will judge you every one after his ways."

Has He given up on Israel or the Jews? Salvation came by the Jews, through Jesus/Yeshua, but they did not receive Him at His first coming. *But when they become believers in Yeshua and then say*, according to

Matthew 23:39 (KJV) "… Blessed is he that cometh in the name of the Lord." *He will return*.

2.15   Once you are divorced are you allowed to remarry?

If, by this question, you mean can a divorced person remarry, then the answer is that a single person has a legal right to remarry. If this question refers to a divorced Christian remarrying, then there is Scripture to consider.

First let us understand about marriage from a Biblical viewpoint and why it was instituted by God. In **Genesis 2:18** we learn that God provided Adam with a helpmate so he would not be lonely. Moreover, Adam was to be in charge of the family unit and Eve was to be a team-player giving (phileo) love to the team. We learn from **Ephesians 5:25, 28, 33** that husbands are commanded to love their wives, but not vice-versa. In **Titus 2:4-5** we learn that the wives are to be taught by the older women *how to love* their husbands. But this love is all about how to play on their husbands' team, evidently something they have not learned elsewhere. Now that the basics have been established, let us consider the original question. In

Luke 16:18 (NIV) "Anyone who divorces his wife and marries another woman commits adultery, and the man who marries a divorced woman commits adultery." So, the true cost of divorce and remarriage is adultery, which is a sin. This is seen in

Galatians 5:19 (NKJ) "Now the works of the flesh are evident, which are: **adultery, fornication,** uncleanness, lewdness," *So the sin of adultery must be repented of in order to enter heaven.*

In **Matthew 19:3**, the Pharisees ask Jesus a question about divorce and we get His answer in **Matthew 19:4-8**, which is that God permitted divorce because of the hardness of men's hearts, but it was not His intent that divorce should occur, because the two have become one. Each had given their virginity to the other, and this can only be given once. God had Moses write in

Deuteronomy 24:1 (NIV) "If a man marries a woman who becomes displeasing to him because he finds something indecent about her, and he writes her a certificate of divorce, gives it to her and sends her from his house", then the marriage has ended. What happens next? *One can either remain single or remarry.*

The Bible gives several reasons for remaining single *either before or after divorce.* Some are given in

I Corinthians 7:1-9 in which fornication might result without being married. The other alternative involves becoming a *eunuch* with the relevant Scriptures being given in

Matthew 19:12 (NKJ) "For there are eunuchs who were born thus from their mother's womb, and there are eunuchs who were made eunuchs by men, and there are eunuchs who have made themselves eunuchs for the kingdom of heaven's sake. He who is able to accept it, let him accept it."

2.16   What does it mean to 'take up your cross and follow me'?

It basically means that you are to consider yourself as a dead man and to follow the leading of Jesus, through the Holy Spirit, on a daily basis. When you are dead to sin and follow the scriptural admonition given in

1 John 2:16 (KJV) "For all that is in the world, the lust of the flesh, and the lust of the eyes, and the pride of life, is not of the Father, but is of the world.", then you have truly taken up your cross and are following Jesus. It is also helpful to remember that

Galatians 2:20 (KJV) "I am crucified with Christ: nevertheless I live; yet not I, but Christ liveth in me: and the life which I now live in the flesh I live by the faith of the Son of God, who loved me, and gave himself for me."

Lastly, we need to remind ourselves that it is hard to insult, taunt, or tempt a dead man.

2.17   Why do some churches not allow women ministers?

Different churches have different traditions; human families do as well. Those churches which do not allow women ministers use as the reason the writing of Paul. In particular,

1 Corinthians 14:34-35 (NIV) "women should remain silent in the churches. They are not allowed to speak, but must be in submission, as the Law says. If they want to inquire about something, they should ask their own husbands at home; for it is disgraceful for a woman to speak in the church." I have been taught that this was so because in the early church times, the men and women sat on opposite sides of the aisle, as in a synagogue. (*However, I have recently learned that the*

Synagogue in Capernaum, in which Jesus worshipped, has been partially reconstructed consistent with the time period of His ministry. From this reconstruction, it has been learned that the women sat in a balcony; whereas, the men sat at the floor level on two/three rows of stone blocks located on opposite sides of the room, facing one another.) Thus, if a woman wanted more understanding about what the speaker was saying, Paul writes for her to just wait until they get home to ask her husband rather than disturb the meeting; otherwise, she would first have to get her husband's attention and then ask him her question. He, in turn, would miss what the speaker was saying next in order to answer her question, which would also be disturbing to others.

However, this is not the only Scripture about women speaking in church. The preceding needs to be coupled with

1 Corinthians 11:5, 10 (NIV) which teaches that "... every woman who prays or prophesies with her head uncovered dishonors her head — it is just as though her head were shaved ... For this reason, and because of the angels, the woman ought to have a sign of authority on her head." This means that a woman could speak in a church setting, but she had to show respect for her husband.

Based on the preceding, each congregation or denomination has to decide for itself how to weigh these two seemingly conflicting requirements. *However, in their deliberations*, these groups must be careful not to forget the large role women played in the establishment of the early Christian church. See, for example, **Acts 16:14** where Lydia is mentioned; **Romans 16:1-2** where Phoebe is commended; and in **2 Timothy 1:5** where the faith of Timothy's mother, Eunice, and his grandmother, Lois, has been passed on to Timothy.

2.18 What is meant by the 'fear of the Lord'?

The following Scriptures address this question:

Job 28:28 (NIV) "And he said to man, '**The fear of the Lord** – that is wisdom, and to shun evil is understanding.'" (See **Job 29:1-25** and **Acts 9:31-43** for examples of the personal and church benefits from fearing the Lord.) More examples are contained in the following Scriptures:

1 Sam 11:7 (KJV) "And he took a yoke of oxen, and hewed them in pieces, and sent them throughout all the coasts of Israel by the hands of messengers, saying, Whosoever cometh not forth after Saul and after Samuel, so shall it be done unto his oxen. And the fear of the LORD fell on the people, and they came out with one consent."

2 Chronicles 17:10 (KJV) "And the fear of the LORD fell upon all the kingdoms of the lands that were round about Judah, so that they made no war against Jehoshaphat."

2 Chronicles 19:7 (KJV) "Wherefore now let the fear of the LORD be upon you; take heed and do it: for there is no iniquity with the LORD our God, nor respect of persons, nor taking of gifts."

2 Chronicles 19:9 (KJV) "And he charged them, saying, Thus shall ye do in the fear of the LORD, faithfully, and with a perfect heart."

Psalms 19:9 (KJV) "The fear of the LORD is clean, enduring for ever: the judgments of the LORD are true and righteous altogether."

Psalms 34:11 (KJV) "Come, ye children, hearken unto me: I will teach you the fear of the LORD."

Psalms 111:10 (KJV) "The fear of the LORD is the beginning of wisdom: a good understanding have all they that do his commandments: his praise endureth for ever."

Proverbs 1:7 (KJV) "The fear of the LORD is the beginning of knowledge: but fools despise wisdom and instruction."

Proverbs 1:29 (KJV) "For that they hated knowledge, and did not choose the fear of the LORD:"

Proverbs 2:5 (KJV) "Then shalt thou understand the fear of the LORD, and find the knowledge of God."

Proverbs 8:13 (KJV) "The fear of the LORD is to hate evil: pride, and arrogancy, and the evil way, and the froward mouth, do I hate."

Proverbs 9:10 (KJV) "The fear of the LORD is the beginning of wisdom: and the knowledge of the holy is understanding."

Proverbs 10:27 (KJV) "The fear of the LORD prolongeth days: but the years of the wicked shall be shortened."

Proverbs 14:26-27 (KJV) "In the fear of the LORD is strong confidence: and his children shall have a place of refuge. The fear of the LORD is a fountain of life, to depart from the snares of death."

Proverbs 15:16 (KJV) "Better is little with the fear of the LORD than great treasure and trouble therewith."

Proverbs 15:33 (KJV) "The fear of the LORD is the instruction of wisdom; and before honour is humility.?"

Proverbs 16:6 (KJV) "By mercy and truth iniquity is purged: and by the fear of the LORD men depart from evil."

Proverbs 19:23 (KJV) "The fear of the LORD tendeth to life: and he that hath it shall abide satisfied; he shall not be visited with evil."

Proverbs 22:4 (KJV) "By humility and the fear of the LORD are riches, and honour, and life."

Proverbs 23:17 (KJV) "Let not thine heart envy sinners: but be thou in the fear of the LORD all the day long."

Isaiah 2:10 (KJV) "Enter into the rock, and hide thee in the dust, for fear of the LORD, and for the glory of his majesty."

Isaiah 2:19 (KJV) "And they shall go into the holes of the rocks, and into the caves of the earth, for fear of the LORD, and for the glory of his majesty, when he ariseth to shake terribly the earth."

Isaiah 2:21 (KJV) "To go into the clefts of the rocks, and into the tops of the ragged rocks, for fear of the LORD, and for the glory of his majesty, when he ariseth to shake terribly the earth."

Isaiah 11:2-3 (KJV) "And the spirit of the LORD shall rest upon him, the spirit of wisdom and understanding, the spirit of counsel and might, the spirit of knowledge and of the fear of the LORD; And shall make him of quick understanding in the fear of the LORD: and he shall not judge after the sight of his eyes, neither reprove after the hearing of his ears:" and

Isaiah 33:6 (KJV) "And wisdom and knowledge shall be the stability of thy times, and strength of salvation: the fear of the LORD is his treasure."

2.19 What is meant by 'ye are gods'?

In **John 10:34-35 (KJV)** "Jesus answered them, Is it not written in your law, I said, Ye are gods? If he called them gods, unto whom the word of God came, and the scripture cannot be broken;" Jesus is referring to those prophets and holy men/women of old through whom God spoke to the people and/or wrote down what He said during the Old Covenant times.

2.20 How can man be 'as a god'?

This is the trap that Satan set for Adam and Eve when they ate of the Tree of Knowledge of Good and Evil. Adam knew fellowship with God as God shared His heart with Adam, but Adam did not know anything except that which God TOLD him. If Adam ate of the fruit of the Tree of Knowledge of Good and Evil, he would be like God and could converse with Him as an EQUAL. They were offered a shortcut to godhood by Satan through the eating of fruit as reported in

Genesis 3:4-5 (KJV) "And the serpent said unto the woman, Ye shall not surely die: For God doth know that in the day ye eat thereof, then your eyes shall be opened, and ye shall be as gods, knowing good and evil." **However, it turned out to be a lie, as there is NO such thing as man becoming a god!!** Unfortunately, if you have believed this lie and then die you are in for a **BIG, UNPLEASANT SURPRISE!!**

2.21 Did Jesus ever have any doubts?

The basic answer is No, since He was involved in the plan for His coming to earth and His necessary part. As we learn from

Revelation 13:8 (NIV) "... *the Lamb that was slain from the creation of the world*." Time has no meaning in the heavenly realm, so even before the world was made, the Godhead had decided that a sacrificial Savior was needed for mankind. Moreover, Jesus did not doubt who He was or the path He was on since He did everything in conjunction with the Father and by direction of the Holy Spirit. Lastly, He never doubted whether or not He would ever sin, as Scripture teaches in

John 8:46 (NIV) "Can any of you prove me guilty of sin? If I am telling the truth, why don't you believe me?" and

Hebrews 4:15 (NIV) "For *we do not* have a high priest who is unable to sympathize with our weaknesses, but we have one who has been tempted in every way, just as we are – yet was without sin."

2.22   Is Islam the correct religion?

No! Islam is a religion made up of parts from other religions. However, the **Koran** does correctly point out that Jesus (Isa) was chosen, anointed, did miracles and knows the way to heaven in *Surah Al-Imran 3:42-55* [5]. No such claims are made in the **Koran** for Mohammed. When asked what his role was, *Surah The Sandhills 46:9* [5] reports that he spoke "Say: I am not the first of the apostles, and I do not know what will be done with me or with you: I do not follow anything but that which is revealed to me, and I am only a plain warner."

2.23   Is everything that happened to me, God's will?

The basic answer is No. Many events occur in our lives because has God given mankind 'free will', which means that we can follow Him or not. If someone, who is against God, gets a gun and shoots you, one cannot blame God for this but the person himself who has yielded his 'free will' to someone or something else. However, even in these 'life events', God can use them for His glory if we seek Him about the consequences and what we can learn from them. It might just be that this interruption in our daily routine is just what we needed to take a new look at our lives and where we are going.

2.24 Is every sin a forgivable sin?

Yes, _except_ those committed against the Holy Spirit. Scriptures teach this in

Matthew 12:31 (NIV) "And so I tell you, every sin and blasphemy will be forgiven men, but the blasphemy against the Spirit will not be forgiven." and

Hebrews 6:4-6 (NIV) "It is impossible for those who have once been enlightened, who have tasted the heavenly gift, who have shared in the Holy Spirit, who have tasted the goodness of the word of God and the powers of the coming age, if they fall away, to be brought back to repentance, because to their loss they are crucifying the Son of God all over again and subjecting him to public disgrace."

However, remember that it is difficult to commit this sin because you are basically attributing the works of Satan to the Holy Spirit, and this is not easily done.

2.25 Is it true that we have to give an account to the Lord if we did not try and restore the person?

The basic premise is that we have to give an account for _everything_ we do while on the earth. This is confirmed by

Romans 14:12 (KJV) "So then every one of us shall give account of himself to God."

If the person who needs restoration is a believer, the Scriptures teach that there is a responsibility for fellow believers to help, as described in

Galatians 6:1 (KJV) "Brethren, if a man be overtaken in a fault, ye which are spiritual, restore such an one in the spirit of meekness; considering thyself, lest thou also be tempted."

2.26   Why is the tongue mightier than the sword?

Physical swords have a physical function and that is to kill, maim, terrorize, or maintain order. The tongue is mightier because it can vocalize *ideas*, and ideas are hard to kill; in fact, the more one tries to kill them the more they spread.

2.27   How should we celebrate Christmas?

We should celebrate the entrance of God into the world, but in a manner that is in keeping with the occasion. Excessive spending and going into debt to buy presents which cannot be afforded is a wrong way. Keep your celebration simple, just as it was in the manger, with family (natural and/or church) and friends enjoying one another's company in the spirit of the season. Most celebrations involve food, but keep that simple too, again not being extravagant or going into debt just to impress people.

2.28   Would God have punished Adam if only Eve had eaten the apple?

This question is one of the most challenging I ever faced. On the surface there is a simple answer, but hidden within this question is a great truth. Adam <u>could have said</u> to Eve that 'You did what God told me NOT to do, so I will put you away and God will make me a new helpmate from another rib so that I can be faithful to God'. *If Adam had done this, he would not have been punished.*

However, we need to remember that **sin** had its origin in heaven and God dealt with it there and cast the rebellious angelic hosts down to earth. But **sin** had not entered into the *human race* until Eve. Based on her action and Adam's hypothesized action of rejecting her, she would have been alone and lived a cursed life – unless she could have been reconciled to Adam. However, if reconciliation with Adam were to have taken place, she could NOT have had reconciliation with God, as that was many years away and only through Christ Jesus. But Adam did not do this and that is the interesting part of this scenario. So, why did Adam not put Eve away?

To get at an understanding, let us re-examine

Genesis 2:24 (KJV) "Therefore shall a man leave his father and his mother, and shall cleave unto his wife: and they shall be one flesh." Though I had heard this Scripture quoted many times at weddings, in my mind I had always reversed it to be 'that the woman would leave her father and mother and shall cleave unto her husband'. I could not understand how a man would leave *his* father and mother, as it made more sense to me for the woman to leave her family and join her husband's family. Obviously, I had it backwards – and this became clear to me as I was pondering **_Question 2.28_**. Moreover, then I had to come to grips with 'Who was the father and mother of Adam', the person to whom this passage is addressed? We learn about the lineage of Adam from

Luke 3:38 (KJV) "... Adam, which was the son of God." So now we know who his father was, but what about his mother. This had to be the Holy Spirit as we see from

Genesis 2:7 (KJV) "And the LORD God formed man of the dust of the ground, and breathed into his nostrils the *breath of life*; and man became a living soul." Since the *Strong's word* for 'breath' denotes 'wind' or 'divine inspiration' and since the Holy Spirit is known to create a 'wind' in

Acts 2:2-4 (NIV) "Suddenly a sound like the blowing of a violent wind came from heaven and filled the whole house where they were sitting. They saw what seemed to be tongues of fire that separated and came to rest on each of them. All of them were filled with the Holy Spirit and began to speak in other tongues as the Spirit enabled them." Therefore, it makes sense that the Holy Spirit acted in the way of a mother to give life to the man, Adam.

Now that we have an understanding of Adam's parentage, let us return to the original question. We remember reading that Adam knew fellowship with God as God shared His heart with Adam, but Adam did not know anything except that which God TOLD him. It was NOT enough for Eve to be deceived by the serpent, but Adam was NOT deceived, as reported in

1 Timothy 2:14 (KJV) "… Adam was not deceived, but the woman being deceived was in the transgression". However, Adam wanted to be with this woman, because of his attachment to her (emotional, intellectual and physical), more than he wanted to be with God, even if punishment – separation from God due to *sin* – sickness and death was the result for the human race! We see this in

1 Corinthians 15:22 (KJV) "For as in Adam all die, even so in Christ shall all be made alive." So, whenever you get sick in body, mind, or spirit, **give thanks to Adam**!

Lastly, God looked on Adam and Eve as a single unit, 'man' as seen in

Genesis 5:2 (NIV) "He created them male and female and blessed them. And when they were created, he called them '**man**.'" Though sin had its origin in heaven until it was cleansed, **the 'man' Adam allowed** it to have dominion on earth!

2.29   Would we be here today if Adam and Eve hadn't sinned?

If the question is 'Would we be here today in *the same condition we are in now*?', the answer is No. However, the overriding truth is that, since God knows the end from the beginning, He is never surprised and has a plan to accomplish His goal for all mankind as well as in each individual life. This is why God made provision for Jesus to enter the world so that we could be redeemed. (According to an undated broadcast sermon of *Dr. D. James Kennedy* on the **Coral Ridge Hour** from the Coral Ridge Presbyterian Church, FL, he says that the Bible can be outlined in the general terms of "**Generation, Degeneration** and **Regeneration**." The book of Genesis encompasses the **Generation,** and documents the start of the **Degeneration**; whereas, the **Regeneration** comes through Jesus Christ.)

2.30   How long have good and evil existed together?

Evil is the absence of good, just as cold is the absence of heat and darkness the absence of light. We do not know in the heavenly realm when evil commenced, only that it is depicted in the person of an angelic being, Lucifer, and he was thrown down to earth as described in

Isaiah 14:12-15 (NKJ) "How you are fallen from heaven, O Lucifer, son of the morning! How you are cut down to the ground, you who weakened the nations! For you have said in your heart: 'I will ascend into heaven, I will exalt my throne above the stars of God; I will also sit on the mount of the congregation on the farthest sides of the north; I will ascend above the heights of the clouds, I will be like the Most High.' Yet you shall be brought down to Sheol, to the lowest depths of the Pit."

Ezekiel 28:12-19 (NIV) "...This is what the Sovereign LORD says: 'You were the model of perfection, full of wisdom and perfect in beauty. You were in Eden, the garden of God; every precious stone adorned you: ruby, topaz and emerald, chrysolite, onyx and jasper, sapphire, turquoise and beryl. Your settings and mountings were made of gold; on the day you were created they were prepared. You were anointed as a guardian cherub, for so I ordained you. You were on the holy mount of God; you walked among the fiery stones. You were blameless in your ways from the day you were created till wickedness was found in you. **Through your widespread trade you were filled with violence, and you sinned. So I drove you in disgrace from the mount of God, and I expelled you, O guardian cherub, from among the fiery stones. Your heart became proud on account of your beauty, and you corrupted your wisdom because of your splendor. So I threw you to the earth**; I made a spectacle of you before kings. By your many sins and dishonest trade you have desecrated your sanctuaries. So I made a fire come out from you, and it consumed you, and I reduced you to ashes on the ground in the sight of all who were watching. All the nations who knew you are appalled at you; you have come to a horrible end and will be no more.'" and

Revelation 12:7-9 (KJV) "... war broke out in heaven: Michael and his angels fought with the dragon [Lucifer]; and the dragon and his angels fought, but they did not prevail, nor was a place found for them in heaven any longer. So the great dragon was cast out, that serpent of old, called the Devil and Satan, who deceives the whole world; he was cast to the earth, and his angels were cast out with him."

We know that now in heaven there is no evil, but on earth there is both good and evil, and all of us must make daily choices about which to follow. Scriptures help us to distinguish the difference, as does the Holy Spirit leadership.

2.31 What is faith? *

There are many definitions of faith, including a variety of Christian traditions and other groups' ideas of getting to heaven. However, the two definitions I like best include "the sufficiency of the evidence" and "trust". With respect to the first, we can never have all the evidence to support any theological position, but what we can substantiate enables us to have the confidence that what we have read and applied works. With respect to "trust", it just says that I believe God will do what He said He will do if I meet the conditions He has set forth. This is just confidence, not in an idea, but in a Person who is supremely trustworthy.

The *Resurrection of Jesus* is a classic example of "the sufficiency of the evidence", as it gave the apostles the boldness to proclaim that **He is alive**, fulfilled relevant prophecies, and is/was the answer to their sin problem.

The classic biblical definition of faith is given in

Hebrews 11:1 (NKJ) "Now faith is the substance of things hoped for, the evidence of things not seen."

2.32 What does God say what you should do with mediums, witches, false prophets?

God addresses this issue in the following Scriptures:

Deuteronomy 18:10-12 (KJV) "There shall not be found among you any one that maketh his son or his daughter to pass through the fire, or that useth divination, or an observer of times, or an enchanter, or a witch, Or a charmer, or a consulter with familiar spirits, or a wizard, or a necromancer. For all that do these things are an abomination unto the LORD: and because of these abominations the LORD thy God doth drive them out from before thee."

Micah 5:12 (KJV) "And I will cut off witchcrafts out of thine hand; and thou shalt have no more soothsayers:"

False Prophets are condemned by God [1] and are defined as "those who falsely claim to utter revelations that come from God, to foretell future events, or to have God's power to produce miracles, signs, and wonders. In the Bible, false prophets fell into three general categories: (1) those who worshiped false gods and served idols; (2) those who falsely claimed to receive messages from the Lord; and (3) those who wandered from the truth and ceased to be true prophets."

2.33 Genesis talks about two creations of man. What's the story?

The first chapter of Genesis deals with the order of the physical development of the universe, whereas the second chapter deals with the relational development of man with God, the creatures, and Eve [6].

2.34 Who is the 'us' in Genesis 1:26; 11:7?

The 'us' referred to has to do with the Godhead: God the Father, God the Son and God the Holy Spirit.

2.35 What is the difference between a Christian and a believer?

To be a real Christian is to be a real believer in the Lord Jesus Christ, so there is *no difference.* Both terms mean that you have had a life-changing experience with Him and He directs your daily life through the power of the Holy Spirit.

2.36   When can you safely add to a scripture?

There is **_no time_** for anyone to safely add to scripture. The most we can hope to do is to understand the Holy Bible with sufficient accuracy so that we can apply it in our lives and conduct. Moreover, we are cautioned in

Revelation 22:18 (NIV) "I warn everyone who hears the words of the prophecy of this book: If anyone **adds anything to them**, God will add to him the plagues described in this book." Not only that, but we are even cautioned about how we read the Bible as given in

2 Peter 1:20 (NIV) "Above all, you must understand that no prophecy of Scripture came about by the prophet's own interpretation." This basically means that no single passage should be read singularly, without its context and without consideration of all other Scriptures that deal with the same matter.

2.37   What are some other names for Jesus in the Bible?

There are so many. Here are a few without the Scriptural citation in the **KJV** from [7]: Adam, Advocate, Almighty, Alpha and Omega, Amen, Angel of his presence, Anointed, Apostle, Arm of the Lord, Author and Finisher of our faith, Beginning and end of the creation of God, Beloved, Blessed and only Potentate, Branch, Bread of life, Bridegroom, Bright and Morning Star, Brightness of the Father's glory, Captain of the Lord's host (army), Captain of Salvation, Carpenter, Chief Shepherd, Chief Cornerstone, Chiefest among ten thousand, Chosen of God, The Christ (Messiah), a King, Christ Jesus our

Lord, Christ of God, the chosen of God, the Son of God, Son of the Blessed, Commander, Consolation of Israel, Cornerstone, Counselor, Covenant of the people, Dayspring, Deliverer, Desire of all nations, the Door, Elect, Emmanuel, Eternal Life, Everlasting Father, Faithful and True, the Faithful and true witness, Finisher of faith, First and last, First begotten of the dead, Foundation, Fountain, Forerunner, Friend of sinners, Gift of God, Glory of Israel, God (deity), God blessed forever, God manifest in the flesh. God of Israel, the Saviour, God of the whole earth, God our Saviour, God's dear Son, God with us, Good Master, Governor, Great Shepherd of the sheep, Head of the ekklesia (body), Heir of all things, High priest, Head of every man, Head of the corner, Holy child Jesus, Holy one of God, Holy thing, (our) Hope, Horn of salvation, I AM, Image of God, Israel, Jehovah, Jehovah's fellow, King of the Jews, Judge, Just man, Just person, Just One, King of Israel, King of the Jews, King of Saints, King of Kings, King of Glory, King of Zion, King over all the earth, Lamb of God, Lawgiver, Leader, Life, Light, Light of the world, Light to the Gentiles, the Living Bread, Living Stone, Lion of the tribe of Judah, Lord, Lord of Lords, Lord of glory, Man of sorrows, Master, the only Mediator, Messenger of the covenant, Messiah the Prince, Mighty God, Mighty one of Israel, Mighty to save, Minister of the sanctuary, Morning Star, Most holy, Most mighty, Offspring of David, Only wise God, our Saviour, Overseer, our Passover, Potentate, Power of God, Physician, Precious Cornerstone, Priest, Prince of Life, Prince of Peace, Prince of the kings of the earth, Prophet, our Sin-offering, Rabbi, Ransom, Redeemer, the Resurrection and the Life, Redemption, Righteous Branch, Righteous Judge, Rock, Root of David, Root of Jesse, Rose of Sharon, Ruler in Israel, Salvation, Sanctification, Sanctuary, Saviour of the world, Sceptre, the Second Man, Seed of David, Seed of the woman, Servant of rulers, Shepherd and Overseer of souls, Shepherd of Israel, Shiloh, Son of the Father, Son of God, Son of Man,

Son of David, Sun of Righteousness, Surety, Stone of Stumbling, Sure Foundation, Teacher, True God, True Vine, Truth, Unspeakable Gift, the Vine, the Way, I AM THAT I AM, Wisdom, the Wisdom of God, Witness, Wonderful, Word of God, and Word of Life.

2.38 Are you always saved, even after you sin? Do you need to be reclaimed/restored?

First of all, being saved means to get you/me out of the sinning business. This is the basic meaning of

I John 3:9 (NIV) "No one who is born of God will continue to sin, because God's seed remains in him; he cannot go on sinning, because he has been born of God." Since the seed of God has entered into us, He messes us up from being the 'good sinner' that we were. However, we can push through the 'hedge of protection' He offers and still sin, but this time it is against our new nature – which is <u>not</u> to sin. So when we do sin, we need to do again what we did to get saved and that is the confession of sin and acceptance of forgiveness. This has been provided for by God in

I John 2:1 (NIV) "My dear children, I write this to you so that you will not sin. But if anybody does sin, we have one who speaks to the Father in our defense – Jesus Christ, the Righteous One."

We also need to take seriously the full meaning of the message given in

Romans 5:6, 8, 10 (NIV) where "You see, at just the right time, when we were still powerless, Christ died for the ungodly…But God demonstrates his own love for us in this: While we were still sinners, Christ died for us…For if, when we were God's enemies, we were reconciled to him through the death of his Son, how much more, having been reconciled, shall we be saved through his life!" *Christ Jesus has taken sinners and made saints out of them, regardless of the standards of the church world.*

2.39 What is the original religion?

The original religion would have been that created by God himself. However, religion is a word that describes man's attempts to reach God and results in a <u>set of rules or bondage</u> instead of freedom. Instead, what God wants is a *relationship* with His people just as He originally had with Adam. During their fellowships in the cool of the evening, God showed Adam His entire plan for salvation detailed in the Zodiac in something called *protoevangelium* [8]. These star groups, whose names we know e.g. *Pisces, Virgo, Scorpio, Leo, etc.*, depict a portion of the Gospel and were told to Adam by God during their walks in the cool of the evening. Adam, in turn, told his sons, Abel, Cain, Seth, etc. Seth is known as the source of the names of the Zodiac among astrologers [8] and those involved in horoscopes, but the **current usage of the Zodiac has been HIJACKED from** its intended purpose. The stars were meant to be a sign which, when read with understanding, were to indicate that something is to happen, including the birth announcement of His Son on earth.

These signs were to be like a thermometer, in that they indicate the temperature but do not cause you to get hot/cold. So, too, the stars are to indicate something is to happen but *do not* cause you to perform in some particular way [9]. We learn from

Genesis 1:14-15 (NKJ) where "… God said, 'Let there be lights in the firmament of the heavens to divide the day from the night; and let them be for *signs and seasons*, and for days and years; and let them be for lights in the firmament of the heavens to give light on the earth'; and it was so."

2.40 Where is the Lord's Prayer found in the Bible?

The Lord's Prayer is found in two different places in the New Testament; namely, **Matthew 6:9-13** and **Luke 11:2-4**, with the one in **Matthew** being more complete. (See answer to *Question 3.20*.)

2.41 Are the Christian God and the sun the same?

No! The Christian God is quite different than the sun. First of all, the Christian God is uncreated, whereas the sun is merely a created star in the Milky Way galaxy. Therefore, God, who created the universe including our solar-system star/sun, cannot be said to be equal to sun, as the creator is vastly superior to the creation.

CHAPTER 3 – CHRISTIAN WALK

3.1   How do you know if your walk with Christ is right?

3.2   How do I know where I am with respect to my walk with Jesus?

3.3   What can we do to help our walk with God?

3.4   How do you know you are running the Lord's race with patience?

3.5   What do I need or what are the things I should do in order to stay on God's path?

3.6   What can we do every day to build our belief in God?

3.7   How do we know that we are doing God's will?

There are two principles on which to build answers to these questions. The first is contained in

Matthew 22:29 (NIV) "Jesus replied, 'You are in error because you do not know the Scriptures or the power of God.'" If we stay out of reading, meditating and understanding God's word, then we miss out on getting His **wisdom**! This **wisdom** will keep us out of trouble, especially when coupled with the leading of the Holy Spirit – identified here as 'the power of God'. The second principle is given in

I John 3:19-22 (NIV) and teaches that "This then is how we know that we belong to the truth, and how we set our hearts at rest in his presence whenever our hearts condemn us. For God is greater than our hearts, and he knows everything. Dear friends, if our hearts do not condemn us, we have confidence before God and receive from him anything we ask, because we obey his commands and do what pleases him."

So, if we are in His presence, then we can be sure we are walking right, are in the right race, on the right path, have the right belief in God, and doing God's will.

3.8 How to stay rooted in the Word?

This is a matter of discipline. If you really want to, you must make it a habit of setting aside some time to read His word and to meditate upon it, because we always have time to do the things we want to do. See the answer to ***Question 5.10*** for more details.

3.9 What happens when we get dry – where is the Lord?

3.10 How to overcome a lack of desire to come to church and to seek God more?

The basic answers are that the Lord is where you left Him and your desire to seek Him diminishes the farther away from Him you stray. Check your life and see if you have forgotten to do what is needed, as contained in the answer to ***Questions 3.1-3.7***.

You can also take confidence in the words of Jesus recorded in

Matthew 28:20 (NIV) "… And surely I am with you always, to the very end of the age." The Lord is with the believer even when he does not recognize His presence.

3.11 Why do I forget about God?

3.12 Why do we take God for granted?

Of course, you are the only one who is able to answer this question completely, but the basic answer for most people is that you are distracted by things/events you consider more important. There are Scriptural examples in which this has occurred before:

Job 8:13 (KJV) "So are the paths of all that forget God; and the hypocrite's hope shall perish:"

Psalms 9:17 (KJV) "The wicked shall be turned into hell, and all the nations that forget God." and

Psalms 50:22 (KJV) "Now consider this, ye that forget God, lest I tear you in pieces, and there be none to deliver."

Taking God for granted is like not remembering Him or forgetting about Him and not involving Him in our lives. We may think of God as a tree that we know is ALWAYS there, observe it, and enjoy its shade without giving any real thought to developing a relationship with it.

3.13 Does God still forgive when we do harmful things, mistreat people? Does He forgive us?

Yes, if we are truly repentant and have had a change of heart. The Christian faith is based on our being sinners, God having a standard of perfection to get to heaven, and His providing a way, through Christ Jesus, by faith in what He did for us. He gives us the gift of Eternal Life as we trust in His redemptive work on the cross.

3.14 If I fear God, why do I sin?

An answer might be that you only "kind of" fear God, knowing that _He will forgive you when you do sin and repent_! But suppose you sin and die before repenting, then what?

(See answer to **Question 3.36**.) However, the _real 'fear of God'_ is covered in the following Scriptures:

Job 28:28 (KJV) "And unto man he said, Behold, the _fear of the Lord_, that is wisdom; and to depart from evil is understanding."

Acts 9:31 (KJV) "Then had the churches rest throughout all Judaea and Galilee and Samaria, and were edified; and walking in the _fear of the Lord_, and in the comfort of the Holy Ghost, were multiplied." and

Deuteronomy 14:23 (KJV) which reports that "And thou shalt eat before the LORD thy God, in the place which he shall choose to place his name there, the tithe of thy corn, of thy wine, and of thine oil, and the firstlings of thy herds and of thy flocks; that thou mayest learn to _fear the LORD_ thy God always."

To this, let us add the wisdom recorded in

James 1:12-15 (KJV) "Blessed is the man that endureth temptation: for when he is tried, he shall receive the crown of life, which the Lord hath promised to them that love him. Let no man say when he is tempted, I am tempted of God: for God cannot be tempted with evil, neither tempteth he any man: But every man is tempted, when he is drawn away of his own lust, and enticed. Then when lust hath conceived, it bringeth forth **sin**: and **sin**, when it is finished, bringeth forth death."

Lastly, a _true fear of God_ will produce an awareness of your position made possible by Christ Jesus as described in

Hebrews 10:14 (NIV) "because by one sacrifice he has made perfect forever those who are being made holy."

(You may also want to check out the answer to ***Question 2.18***.)

3.15 *Is it against God's will to drink alcohol?*

The basic answer is No. Remember that in those days, they did not have the medicines we have today. The basics included wine, typically watered down, and olive oil. Paul even wrote in

1 Timothy 5:23 (NIV) to "Stop drinking only water, and use a little wine because of your stomach and your frequent illnesses."

What is forbidden and has eternal consequences is drunkenness and partying, etc., as noted in

Luke 21:34 (NIV) "Be careful, or your hearts will be weighed down with dissipation, drunkenness and the anxieties of life, and that day will close on you unexpectedly like a trap."

Romans 13:13-14 (NIV) "Let us behave decently, as in the daytime, not in orgies and drunkenness, not in sexual immorality and debauchery, not in dissension and jealousy. Rather, clothe yourselves with the Lord Jesus Christ, and do not think about how to gratify the desires of the sinful nature."

1 Timothy 3:8 (NIV) "Deacons, likewise, are to be men worthy of respect, sincere, not indulging in much wine, and not pursuing dishonest gain." and

Galatians 5:21 (NIV) "… envy; drunkenness, orgies, and the like. I warn you, as I did before, that <u>those who live like this will not inherit the kingdom of God</u>."

3.16 How [do you] open you heart whole-heartedly to God?

3.17 What is the proper way to give your soul to God?

Be *honest and open* with God and say that you have violated His laws, commandments and will, but that you WANT to change NOW and to follow His leadership. Ask for forgiveness in the name of Jesus and He will forgive your sins and accept you into His family.

Do not play games with God and do not use *excuses*, as this will not accomplish the giving of yourself to God.

3.18 Will I ever be strong enough to go over the mountain and not just go around the mountain?

Yes, you can if you stay close to Him and follow the leading of the Holy Spirit, as detailed in the following Scriptures:

Galatians 5:16 (NIV) "So I say, live by the Spirit, and you will not gratify the desires of the sinful nature."

Philippians 4:13 (NIV) "I can do everything through him who gives me strength." and

1 Corinthians 6:19-20 (NIV) "Do you not know that your body is a temple of the Holy Spirit, who is in you, whom you have received from God? You are not your own; you were bought at a price. Therefore honor God with your body."

Also, see the answers to ***Questions 3.1-3.7***.

3.19 How do we know if we have true repentance?

Use the following Scripture as a test to know whether or not you have truly repented. We read in

I John 3:19-22 (NIV) "This then is how we know that we belong to the truth, and how we set our hearts at rest in his presence whenever our hearts condemn us. For God is greater than our hearts, and he knows everything. Dear friends, if our hearts do not condemn us, we have confidence before God and receive from him anything we ask, because we obey his commands and do what pleases him."

3.20 What is the proper way to pray?

The prayer that Jesus taught His disciples to pray is a good one to start with and is located in

Matthew 6:9-13 (KJV) "After this manner therefore pray ye: Our Father which art in heaven, Hallowed be thy name. Thy kingdom come. Thy will be done in earth, as it is in heaven. Give us this day our daily bread. And forgive us our debts, as we forgive our debtors. And lead us not into temptation, but deliver us from evil: For thine is the kingdom, and the power, and the glory, for ever. Amen." After you have prayed this prayer, have understood its meaning, and have been trying to live the prayer over a period of time; then you may find some Christian books on prayer, as well as reading the words (lyrics) of Christian hymns, to be useful.

3.21 How do we activate our faith?

Activating our faith is not hard but it does seem to be at times. Basically, just trust God and believe He will do what is in the Bible. Some _really good news_ about getting enough faith to receive salvation is found in

Ephesians 2:8-9 (KJV) "For by grace are ye saved through faith; and that not of yourselves: it is the <u>***gift of God:***</u> Not of works, lest any man should boast." This means that all the faith needed to receive the free gift of eternal life is given by God. Start there and trust God to do the rest.

Some very practical steps to activating faith are to: read and meditate upon the Word of God (See the answers to ***Question 5.10***), soak in the Word, and act on it. Remember during this time that God wants to show you how much He *loves you* and that it is **unconditional** through Christ Jesus.

3.22 Should I live under the old covenant or just under the new covenant?

3.23 Should I live under the Law of the Old Covenant or just be under the New Covenant?

We need to live under the New Covenant because the Old Covenant or Law was done away with, as described in

Ephesians 2:15-16(KJV) "Having abolished in his flesh the enmity, <u>*even the law of commandments contained in ordinances;*</u> for to make in himself of twain one new man, so making peace; And that he might reconcile both unto God in one body by the cross, having slain the enmity thereby:"

Moreover, we read in

John 1:17 (KJV) "For the law was given by Moses, but grace and truth came by Jesus Christ." and in

Colossians 2:14 (KJV) "Blotting out the handwriting of ordinances that was against us, which was contrary to us, and took it out of the way, nailing it to his cross;" and in

Galatians 3:24-26 (KJV) "Wherefore the law was our schoolmaster to bring us unto Christ, that we might be justified by faith. But after that faith is come, we are no longer under a schoolmaster. For ye are all the children of God by faith in Christ Jesus."

Even though the Ten Commandments were dealt with in the flesh of Jesus Christ, nine of these are repeated in the New Testament. The first commandment is restated in **Matthew 22:37**, the second is reaffirmed in **1 John 5:21**, the third is embodied in **Colossians 3:8**, the fourth is missing, the fifth is restated in **Ephesians 6:2,3**, and the sixth through the tenth are repeated and reaffirmed in **Romans 13:8-10**. (See also, **Matthew 5:27,28 & 5:21,22**.) The missing commandment is that regarding the Sabbath day. [10]

3.24 How can we keep from letting religion [Christianity] being too complicated?

By trusting God, reading and following the teachings in the Bible, and being led by the Holy Spirit. If you do these things, your relationship with God will not be complicated and your Christianity will be **_real_**. See the answer to **_Questions 3.1-3.7_** for more details.

3.25 How does flattery hurt one's walk with Christ?

It can be detrimental if you allow yourself to think that the comments are due to you alone. This can lead to pride, which can lead to problems, as explained in

Proverbs 16:18 (KJV) "Pride goeth before destruction, and a haughty spirit before a fall."

The best thing to do when flattered is to say "Praise be to God!" This gives God whatever glory is due for that which prompted the flattery.

3.26 How do we know what is God's personal will for your life, i.e. spiritual gifting?

There are two basic answers to this question. The first is that the spiritual gifting is revealed to a prophet/prophetess in a prayer meeting, who in turn shares this information with you. The second method is to realize that God has equipped each of us separately with talents, abilities, skills for His glory. More than that, He will even plant the desire in our hearts to do a particular thing and we will agree that this is what we should do. Beyond that, we grow into our *spiritual gifting* by practicing the simple things of our faith. The latter is more fully explained in [11].

3.27 How can you help someone who is convinced that they don't need any emotional or spiritual help?

The only thing that you may be able to do is to pray for that person and encourage him in the Lord. (**P**ray **U**ntil **S**omething **H**appens – **PUSH**.) More than that, you can tell the person that he appeared troubled and offer to speak with him privately. If that is refused, then just say you will pray God will help him to overcome the situation. (During your private prayer time, you intercede for him and also command that his spiritual eyes be opened by the *authority and power* of Jesus Christ.) However, if the person is open to a Bible study or conversation, then ask the Holy Spirit to direct the study/conversation in such a way as this person will see their need for help.

3.28 Is it okay to repeatedly pray for something, or is one time sufficient?

3.29 What would it be if you pray for something more than once? Is this lack of faith?

3.30 Does God bless us in the long term by not answering some prayers?

3.31 How to reconcile: 'Pray without ceasing' with 'Have faith in your prayer that it will be answered'?

Let us look at these two concepts about prayer. The first is found in

1Thessolonians 5:16-18 (KJV) "Rejoice evermore. Pray without ceasing. In every thing give thanks: for this is the will of God in Christ Jesus concerning you." So we learn from this that we are to be in constant prayer, or have a prayer attitude and give thanks for everything that comes our way.

The second concept is described in

John 14:13-14 (KJV) "And whatsoever ye shall ask in my name, that will I do, that the Father may be glorified in the Son. If ye shall ask any thing in my name, I will do it." However, this must be balanced with

I John 5:14-15 (KJV) "And this is the confidence that we have in him, that, if we ask any thing according to his will, he heareth us: And if we know that he hear us, whatsoever we ask, we know that we have the petitions that we desired of him."

So now we have the whole picture. If our prayers are in accordance with His will, He will do it; and while we are waiting for the appearance of the answer-to-prayer, we continue to pray with thanksgiving because the answer is on its way. Remember, that many times the things we pray for involve changing other people or ourselves and if God were to completely grant the request at the time it was prayed, this may either violate someone's free will, which He will not do, or overwhelm us.

3.32 How to approach your brother in the Lord who is in sin?

3.33 How to be a 'brother' to one who has become unlovable?

First of all, pray and ask God how to direct you and the conversation. After that, be sure to follow the rules laid out in Scripture, including:

Matthew 18:15-17 (KJV) "Moreover if thy brother shall trespass against thee, go and tell him his fault between thee and him alone: if he shall hear thee, thou hast gained thy brother. But if he will not hear thee, then take with thee one or two more, that in the mouth of two or three witnesses every word may be established. And if he shall neglect to hear them, tell it unto the church: but if he neglects to hear the church, let him be unto thee as a heathen man and a publican."

Galatians 6:1-2 (KJV) "Brethren, if a man be overtaken in a fault, ye which are spiritual, restore such an one in the spirit of meekness; considering thyself, lest thou also be tempted. Bear ye one another's burdens, and so fulfil the law of Christ"

II Thessalonians 3:6 (KJV) "Now we command you, brethren, in the name of our Lord Jesus Christ, that ye withdraw yourselves from every brother that walketh disorderly, and not after the tradition which he received of us."

II Thessalonians 3:14-15 (KJV) "And if any man obey not our word by this epistle, note that man, and have no company with him, that he may be ashamed. Yet count him not as an enemy, but admonish him as a brother."

Also, remember that you, too, were once unlovable and outside of Christ. Be patient with one another. You may also want to see the answers to **Question 3.34**.

3.34　How to reconcile 'bringing people to Christ' with 'minding your own business'?

First of all, consider being a friend to others – showing yourself <u>friendly</u>. Scripture teaches in

Proverbs 18:24 (KJV) that "A man that hath friends must shew himself friendly: and there is a friend that sticketh closer than a brother." Also, Jesus was known as a friendly person without becoming entangled in anything sinful himself. See

Matthew 11:19 (KJV) "The Son of man came eating and drinking, and they say, Behold a man gluttonous, and a winebibber, a friend of publicans and sinners. But wisdom is justified of her children." Observe the attitude of Jesus as reported in

Matthew 9:13 (KJV) "But go ye and learn what that meaneth, I will have mercy, and not sacrifice: for I am not come to call the righteous, but sinners to repentance."

Therefore, build a relationship with the person and be there for him. Then at the right time, he will listen to you because you have earned the right to be heard and believed. However, being friendly to others does not mean that we forget the warning in

James 4:4 (KJV) "Ye adulterers and adulteresses, know ye not that the friendship of the world is enmity with God? whosoever therefore will be a *friend of the world* is the enemy of God." This passage is better understood as we read about *who is over this world* in the words of Jesus as recorded in

John 14:30 (KJV) "Hereafter I will not talk much with you: for the *prince of this world* cometh, and hath nothing in me."

3.35 What is so scary about coming to church?

There are two basic answers. The first is that you may meet God there and He will bring you under conviction of how you are living your life and show you the eternal consequences. These consequences can be **scary**. Another way this can happen is that a prophet or someone operating prophetically may come up to you and tell you about your life – in detail – and warn you of the consequences.

The second answer could be that the other congregational members, in the church you attend, will judge and condemn you for your past behavior. Some of this is to be expected, but the real Christians will welcome you back as a 'Prodigal Son'.

3.36 Why do you think it is good to have downfalls when walking with Jesus?

No! It is not good to sin or have downfalls after becoming a believer, as this means we take our eyes off the prize, Christ Jesus, and Satan wins a round. Also, if we die in that condition the results can have eternal consequences. [*We know that God did give space for repentance (See* **Revelation 2:20-21***) to someone named Jezebel; and if He did it for her, He will do it for you.*] However, having downfalls is a reminder that we are not as sensitive to our share of the suffering of Christ Jesus as we need to be, since we have added to our share by this new sin. Therefore, we need to repent quickly and come back to Him with a humble heart. This process is described in

1 John 2:1(KJV) "My little children, these things write I unto you, that ye sin not. And if any man sin, we have an advocate with the Father, Jesus Christ the righteous:"

Lastly, don't grow cold in the things of the Lord. Don't be backsliding while trying to go forward. This process is written about in

Proverbs 14:14(KJV) "The *backslider in heart shall be filled with his own ways*: and a good man shall be satisfied from himself."

3.37 What are the responsibilities of a Christian?

3.38 How to be a Christian husband?

3.39 How can I encourage my wife in God and to follow church and to raise children in God without forcing it on her?

The answers to these questions are detailed in the following Scriptures in that, as a Christian, I have responsibilities to many: to God, my wife, my children, to fellow believers, to those outside the Body of Christ, and to myself.

<u>1-To God:</u>

Matthew 22:37 (NAS) "Love God with whole heart, mind and strength"

1 Peter 5:6 (NAS) "Humble yourselves, therefore, under the mighty hand of God, that He may exalt you at the proper time" and

James 4:15 (NAS) "Instead, {you ought} to say, 'If the Lord wills, we shall live and also do this or that.'"

2-To Wife:

Ephesians 5:25 (NAS) "Husbands, love your wives, just as Christ also loved the church and gave Himself up for her;"

Ephesians 5:33 (NAS) "Nevertheless let each individual among you also love his own wife even as himself; and {let} the wife {see to it} that she respect her husband."

1 Peter 3:7 (NAS) "You husbands likewise, live with {your wives} in an understanding way, as with a weaker vessel, since she is a woman; and grant her honor as a fellow heir of the grace of life, so that your prayers may not be hindered." and

1 Corinthians 13:4-7 (NAS) "Love is patient, love is kind, {and} is not jealous; love does not brag {and} is not arrogant, does not act unbecomingly; it does not seek its own, is not provoked, does not take into account a wrong {suffered,} does not rejoice in unrighteousness, but rejoices with the truth; bears all things, believes all things, hopes all things, endures all things."

3-To Children:

Proverbs 22:6 (NAS) "Train up a child in the way he should go, even when he is old he will not depart from it." and

Ephesians 6:4 (NAS) "... fathers, do not provoke your children to anger; but bring them up in the discipline and instruction of the Lord."

Also, worship God at home and with the children, helping them to develop a 'taste' for the things of God. Also, take them to Sunday School and church.

4-To Fellow Believers:

Matthew 22:39 (NAS) "...Love your neighbor as yourself"

John 13:34 (NAS) "... that you love one another, even as I have loved you"

John 17:26 (NAS) "... that the love wherewith Thou didst love Me may be in them..."

Romans 12:10 (NAS) "Be devoted to one another in brotherly love; give preference to one another in honor;" and

Romans 14:14-18 (NAS) "I know and am convinced in the Lord Jesus that nothing is unclean in itself; but to him who thinks anything to be unclean, to him it is unclean. For if because of food your brother is hurt, you are no longer walking according to love. Do not destroy with your food him for whom Christ died. Therefore do not let what is for you a good thing be spoken of as evil; for the kingdom of God is not eating and drinking, but righteousness and peace and joy in the Holy Spirit. For he who in this {way} serves Christ is acceptable to God and approved by men."

<u>5-To Those outside the body of Christ:</u>

Luke 6:27 (NAS) teaches that we are to "... love your enemies, do good to those who hate you,"

<u>6-To Oneself:</u>

2 Timothy 2:15 (NAS) "Be diligent to present yourself approved to God as a workman who does not need to be ashamed, handling accurately the word of truth."

Matthew 6:33 (NAS) "But seek first His kingdom and His righteousness; and all these things shall be added to you."

Galatians 5:16 (NAS) "But I say, walk by the Spirit, and you will not carry out the desire of the flesh."

1 Peter 1:16 (NAS) "because it is written, 'You shall be holy, for I am holy.'" and

Galatians 5:22-26 (NAS) "But the fruit of the Spirit is love, joy, peace, patience, kindness, goodness, faithfulness, gentleness, self-control; against such things there is no law. Now those who belong to Christ Jesus have crucified the flesh with its passions and desires. If we live by the Spirit, let us also walk by the Spirit. Let us not become boastful, challenging one another, envying one another."

3.40 How [do I] really forgive people and move on?

The basic message is that you really have *no choice but to forgive people and move on unless you want to face the eternal consequences.* Remember that forgiveness is a **decision**, not a **feeling**. Let us examine some examples and Scriptures.

<u>What did Jesus do?</u>

Luke 23:34 (KJV) "Then said Jesus, 'Father, **forgive** them; for they know not what they do.' And they parted his raiment, and cast lots."

<u>What did Jesus tell the apostles and us to do?</u>

Matthew 6:12-15 (KJV) "And **forgive** us our debts, as we **forgive** our debtors. And lead us not into temptation, but deliver us from evil: For thine is the kingdom, and the power, and the glory, for ever. Amen. For if ye **forgive** men their trespasses, your heavenly Father will also **forgive** you: But if ye **forgive** not men their trespasses, neither will your Father **forgive** your trespasses."

Matthew 18:21 (KJV) "Then came Peter to him, and said, 'Lord, how oft shall my brother sin against me, and I **forgive** him? till seven times?'"

Matthew 18:35(KJV) "<u>So likewise shall my heavenly Father do also unto you, if ye from your hearts forgive not every one his brother their trespasses.</u>"

Mark 11:25-26 (KJV) "And when ye stand praying, **forgive**, if ye have ought against any: that your Father also which is in heaven may **forgive** you your trespasses. But if ye do not **forgive**, neither will your Father which is in heaven **forgive** your trespasses."

Luke 17:3-4 (KJV) "Take heed to yourselves: If thy brother trespass against thee, rebuke him; and if he repent, **forgive** him. And if he trespass against thee seven times in a day, and seven times in a day turn again to thee, saying, I repent; thou shalt **forgive** him." and

I John 1:8-10 (KJV) "If we say that we have no sin, we deceive ourselves, and the truth is not in us. If we confess our sins, he is faithful and just to **forgive** us our sins, and to cleanse us from all unrighteousness. If we say that we have not sinned, we make him a liar, and his word is not in us."

CHAPTER 4 – ON DEATH

4.1 *What happens after death?* *

4.2 *What happens to our soul when we die? Can we go to heaven now or when Christ returns?*

4.3 *If we were to die today, would our spirit (soul) go to heaven... or do we wait in the grave for Jesus Christ's coming again?*

4.4 *Do we go to heaven right when we die or do we have to rest in the ground?*

There are several options (opinions) given among men. They include: you cease to exist, you rest in the grave, you get reincarnated, you become part of the universal soul, or you go to be with the Lord immediately. To these we will look at what Jesus said about this question and the role of demons. They will be discussed in this order.

You cease to exist is the evolutionary viewpoint; it considers us to be just like other creatures/animals.

You rest in the grave until Jesus comes to get you is based on **Daniel 12:1-2 (KJV)** "And at that time shall Michael stand up, the great prince which standeth for the children of thy people: and there shall be a time of trouble, such as never was since there was a nation even to that same time: and at that time thy people shall be delivered, every one that shall be found written in the book. And many of them that <u>sleep in the dust of the earth shall awake</u>, some to everlasting life, and some to shame and everlasting contempt."

However, the dead know nothing, as recorded in

Ecclesiastes 9:5 (KJV) "For the living know that they shall die: but **the dead know not any thing**, neither have they any more a reward; for the memory of them is forgotten." This is consistent with the soul leaving the body [the soul contains the intellect, emotions and will (this includes memory)] as noted in

Genesis 35:18-19 (KJV) "And it came to pass, as **her soul was in departing, (for she died)** that she called his name Benoni: but his father called him Benjamin. And Rachel died, and was buried in the way to Ephrath, which is Bethlehem."

You get reincarnated is unsupported by Scripture because

Hebrews 9:27 (KJV) reports that "And as it is appointed unto men once to die, but after this the judgment:" **_Resurrection and reincarnation cannot both be true_**.

You become a part of the universal soul is unsupported by Scripture and is associated with Eastern religions & New Age teachings.

You get to be with the Lord immediately has a Scriptural basis and it is

2 Corinthians 5:6-8 (KJV) "Therefore we are always confident, knowing that, whilst we are at home in the body, we are absent from the Lord: (For we walk by faith, not by sight:) We are confident, I say, and willing rather *to be absent from the body, and to be present with the Lord*."

What Jesus said about this question is contained in

Matthew 22:32 (KJV) "I am the God of Abraham, and the God of Isaac, and the God of Jacob? God is not the God of the dead, but of the living." Therefore, those that die in God have their *spirit bodies* present with Him now and they are alive.

The role of demons is that they are used to trick the 'unsuspecting' or 'those pre-conditioned' into accepting messages 'about a prior life' or from 'beyond the grave'. Some groups call the latter a 'testimony'. Mormons and Buddhists, among others, are susceptible to these spirits. The fundamental truth here is **there is no memory before birth**, so a child cannot report past events or recount a prior life. Also, the Bible is quite clear about dealing with 'the spirits of the dead', as recorded in

Leviticus 20:6 (KJV) "And the soul that turneth after such as have familiar spirits, and after wizards, to go a whoring after them, I will even set my face against that soul, and will cut him off from among his people."

An interesting observation is what happens to those who have been declared clinically dead but resuscitated. Many report seeing a bright light and those who have had allegiance to Christ Jesus go on to visit heaven, while others who have not trusted Jesus report a fiery heat. You judge what is real; men's opinions, the Words of Jesus and those who have been close to death but returned, plus the testimony of dying Christians.

4.5 *Are people that do good and believe in God, but not Jesus, going to Hell?*

Let us begin by noting that going to hell is the same as missing heaven. Therefore, what does it take to get to heaven? This is the real question. The following Scriptures answer this question:

John 3:36 (KJV) "He that believeth on the Son hath everlasting life: and he that believeth not the Son shall not see life; but the wrath of God abideth on him."

John 10:30 (KJV) "I and my Father are one."

John 14:1 (KJV) "Let not your heart be troubled: ye believe in God, believe also in me."

Acts 4:10-12 (KJV) "Be it known unto you all, and to all the people of Israel, that by the name of Jesus Christ of Nazareth, whom ye crucified, whom God raised from the dead, even by him doth this man stand here before you whole. This is the stone which was set at nought of you builders, which is become the head of the corner. **Neither is there salvation in any other**: for there is none other name under heaven given among men, whereby we must be saved."

Romans 9:11(KJV) "(For the children being not yet born, neither having done any good or evil, that the purpose of God according to election might stand, not of works, but of him that calleth;)"

Ephesians 2:8-10 (KJV) "For by grace are ye saved through faith; and that not of yourselves: it is the gift of God: Not of works, lest any man should boast. For we are his workmanship, created in Christ Jesus unto good works, which God hath before ordained that we should walk in them."

1Thessalonians 5:9(KJV) "For God hath not appointed us to wrath, but to obtain salvation by our Lord Jesus Christ,"

Titus 1:3-4(KJV) "But hath in due times manifested his word through preaching, which is committed unto me according to the commandment of God our Saviour; To Titus, mine own son after the common faith: Grace, mercy, and peace, from God the Father and the Lord Jesus Christ our Saviour."

Titus 2:10...2:13 (KJV) "Not purloining, but shewing all good fidelity; that they may adorn the doctrine of God our Saviour in all things. Looking for that blessed hope, and the glorious appearing of the great God and our Saviour Jesus Christ;"

Titus 3:4-6 (KJV) "But after that the kindness and love of God our Saviour toward man appeared, Not by works of righteousness which we have done, but according to his mercy he saved us, by the washing of regeneration, and renewing of the Holy Ghost; Which he shed on us abundantly through Jesus Christ our Saviour;" and

1 Peter 1:8-11 (KJV) "Whom having not seen, ye love; in whom, though now ye see him not, yet believing, ye rejoice with joy unspeakable and full of glory: Receiving the end of your faith, even the salvation of your souls. Of which salvation the prophets have inquired and searched diligently, who prophesied of the grace that should come unto you: Searching what, or what manner of time the Spirit of Christ which was in them did signify, when it testified beforehand the sufferings of Christ, and the glory that should follow."

4.6 What about the people who lived before Jesus died?

4.7 What about the people who died before Jesus died?

These two questions yield the same result. If they believed in God and were living for Him, then they were classified as 'Old Testament saints' and, when they died, their souls went to Paradise. This is covered by the following passage in

Luke 16:19-26 (NKJ) "There was a certain rich man who was clothed in purple and fine linen and fared sumptuously every day. But there was a certain beggar named Lazarus, full of sores, who was laid at his gate, desiring to be fed with the crumbs which fell from the rich man's table. Moreover the dogs came and licked his sores. So it was that the beggar died, and was carried by the angels to Abraham's bosom. The rich man also died and was buried. And being in torments in Hades, he lifted up his eyes and saw Abraham [*in Paradise*] afar off, and Lazarus in his bosom. Then he cried and said, 'Father Abraham, have mercy on me, and send Lazarus that he may dip the tip of his finger in water and cool my tongue; for I am tormented in this flame.' But Abraham said, 'Son, remember that in your lifetime you received your good things, and likewise Lazarus evil things; but now he is comforted and you are tormented. And besides all this, between us and you there is a great gulf fixed, so that those who want to pass from here to you cannot, nor can those from there pass to us.'"

Therefore, those 'Old Testament saints' waited in Paradise until the time when Jesus died and took them to heaven with Him. This is covered by the following Scripture:

Ephesians 4:8 (NKJ) "Therefore He says: 'When He ascended on high, he led captivity captive, and gave gifts to men.'" These captives were those in Paradise who went with Jesus when He went to Heaven to put His own blood on the heavenly Mercy Seat. Paradise has now been relocated to Heaven and declared by

Revelation 2:7 (NKJ) "'... He who has an ear, let him hear what the Spirit says to the churches. To him who overcomes I will give to eat from the tree of life, which is in the midst of the Paradise of God.'"

It should be pointed out that the preceding is a different process from what happens to the physical body of the dead saints when the Lord Jesus returns, as described in

1 Thessalonians 4:15-17 (NKJ) "For this we say to you by the word of the Lord, that we who are alive and remain until the coming of the Lord will by no means precede those who are asleep. For the Lord Himself will descend from heaven with a shout, with the voice of an archangel, and with the trumpet of God. And the dead in Christ will rise first.

Then we who are alive and remain shall be caught up together with them in the clouds to meet the Lord in the air. And thus we shall always be with the Lord."

We also need to keep in mind what Jesus said about God (the Father) as recorded in

John 10:30 (KJV) "I and my Father are one."

If those who lived or died before Jesus died, and did so without believing in and living for God, their eternal destiny was settled as it is now for those who live the same way.

4.8 *How are the mentally retarded judged by God?*

First of all, we can be assured that God will judge justly and take into account those who have mental problems. Remember what is reported in

Luke 23:34 (KJV) "Then said Jesus, Father, *forgive them; for they know not what they do*. And they parted his raiment, and cast lots."

However, we, on the other hand, need to be careful about our own judging. Jesus says in **Matthew 7:1-6 (NIV)** & **Luke 6:36-42 (NIV)** to be merciful. Don't bind yourself by condemning others. And yet, if we have been careful in examining ourselves and our motives and **still** find that there is something to say to correct a situation, we **still** need to realize that our words may be considered as 'pearls before a pig', which words will then **not** be valued by them...and they may in turn attack **you**. *What we say and when we say it is important!*

Moreover, whatever you ***GIVE*** will be multiplied and given back to you, be ***IT*** mercy, judgment, condemnation or forgiveness. Note that a plank in your own eye – even a speck in your eye causes a distorted view – blinds a person to see clearly what is in another's eye. **(Matthew 7:3 (NKJ))**

4.9   What would heaven be like? What is its magnitude?

Heaven is indescribable, but Holy and personable. We learn from

Ephesians 2:6-7 (KJV) "And hath raised us up together, and made us sit together in heavenly places in Christ Jesus: That in the ***ages to come*** he might shew the exceeding riches of his grace in his kindness toward us through Christ Jesus." I think God will reveal all those times He interacted with us while we were on earth and expand our understanding of what He was able to do, using us. The term "ages to come" is an enormous amount of time in which He will show us His kindness to us.

Magnitude in the spiritual realm is not a limiting factor as it is in the physical realm. In the heavenly realm, only time is important and it is always NOW.

4.10   Will you be ready when the Lord returns?

The Lord is coming again, as stated in

John 14:3 (KJV) "And if I go and prepare a place for you, I will come again, and receive you unto myself; that where I am, there ye may be also." and

John 14:28 (KJV) "Ye have heard how I said unto you, I go away, and come again unto you. If ye loved me, ye would rejoice, because I said, I go unto the Father: for my Father is greater than I."

The only question is: Have you prepared yourself for His return? Will He find you looking for His return and expecting it to occur, or have you forgotten about this soon coming event and are busy with your own life?

Chapter 5 – How to Hear from God

5.1 How do you know that you are being directed by God to do something?

5.2 How do you know when the Holy Spirit is talking to you?

5.3 How do you know if the Holy Spirit is dwelling in you?

5.4 How to realize your spiritual gift and how to use it accordingly?

5.5 How do you know if you are called to preach?

5.6 How does one find God's will or calling for his life?

5.7 How do you know if you have a calling on your life? Do you get a sign?

5.8 How do we know that revelations a person receives are from God?

5.9 How do you know that God is speaking to your heart?

First of all, there are many wonderful books written by Christian men and women who address one or more of these nine questions in detail. These books can be found in many Christian and secular bookstores. However, some general statements can be made about 'hearing from God' and 'the call on your life'. Let us keep in mind

Jeremiah 29:11 (NIV) "'… For I know the plans I have for you,' declares the LORD, 'plans to prosper you and not to harm you, plans to give you hope and a future.'" Since the

Lord has plans for us, it is reasonable to assume that He wants to communicate them to us; otherwise, we will have no idea what we are to do for Him. Suppose He decides to keep His plans for us a **_secret_**. Then we will never know what these are; but, since He wants the best for us, I am convinced He broadcasts these to us daily in various ways and in varying degrees so that we are not overwhelmed all at once by the full extent of the plan.

Regarding 'the call on your life', we are all called to be the sons of God by virtue of the sacrificial death of Christ Jesus. Once we have repented and become believers, then we are open to more specific callings on our lives. But first let us do the simple things such as 'excusing one another' [**Romans 2:15 (KJV)**], 'preferring one another' [**Romans 12:10 (KJV)**], 'forgiving one another' [**Ephesians 4:32 (KJV)**], 'love one another' [**1 John 4:7 (KJV)**], etc. Doing these simple things, required of all believers, will prepare you for the specific plan God has for you.

Concerning the specific giftings you have been given, search out the following Scriptures for detailed information:

Romans 12:1-21 (NKJ) "I beseech you therefore, brethren, by the mercies of God, that you present your bodies a living sacrifice, holy, acceptable to God, which is your reasonable service. And do not be conformed to this world, but be transformed by the renewing of your mind, that you may prove what is that good and acceptable and perfect will of God. For I say, through the grace given to me, to everyone who is among you, not to think of himself more highly than he ought to think, but to think soberly, as God has dealt to each one a measure of faith. For as we have many members in one body, but all the members do not have the same function, so we, being many, are one body in Christ, and individually members of one another. Having then gifts differing according to the grace that is given to us, let us use them: if prophecy, let us prophesy in proportion to our faith; or ministry, let us use it in our ministering; he who teaches, in teaching; he who exhorts, in exhortation; he who gives, with liberality; he who leads, with diligence; he who shows mercy, with cheerfulness. Let love be without hypocrisy. Abhor what is evil. Cling to what is good. Be kindly affectionate to one another with brotherly love, in honor giving preference to one another; not lagging in diligence, fervent in spirit, serving the Lord; rejoicing in hope, patient in tribulation, continuing steadfastly in prayer; distributing to the needs of the saints, given to hospitality. Bless those who persecute you; bless and do not curse. Rejoice with those who rejoice, and weep with those who weep. Be of the same mind toward one another. Do not set your mind on high things, but associate with the humble. Do not be wise in your own opinion. Repay no one evil for evil. Have regard for good things in the sight of all men. If it is possible, as much as depends on you, live peaceably with all men. Beloved, do not avenge yourselves, but rather give place to wrath; for it is written, 'Vengeance is Mine, I will repay,' says the Lord. Therefore 'If your enemy is hungry, feed him; if he is thirsty, give him a drink; for in so doing you will heap coals of fire on his head.' Do not be overcome by evil, but overcome evil with good."

1 Corinthians 12:1-31 (NKJ) "Now concerning spiritual gifts, brethren, I do not want you to be ignorant: You know that you were Gentiles, carried away to these dumb idols, however you were led. Therefore I make known to you that no one speaking by the Spirit of God calls Jesus accursed, and no one can say that Jesus is Lord except by the Holy Spirit. There are diversities of gifts, but the same Spirit. There are differences of ministries, but the same Lord. And there are diversities of activities, but it is the same God who works all in all. But the manifestation of the Spirit is given to each one for the profit of all: for to one is given the word of wisdom through the Spirit, to another the word of knowledge through the same Spirit, to another faith by the same Spirit, to another gifts of healings by the same Spirit, to another the working of miracles, to another prophecy, to another discerning of spirits, to another different kinds of tongues, to another the interpretation of tongues. But one and the same Spirit works all these things, distributing to each one individually as He wills. For as the body is one and has many members, but all the members of that one body, being many, are one body, so also is Christ. For by one Spirit we were all baptized into one body – whether Jews or Greeks, whether slaves or free – and have all been made to drink into one Spirit. For in fact the body is not one member but many. If the foot should say, 'Because I am not a hand, I am not of the body,' is it therefore not of the body? And if the ear should say, 'Because I am not an eye, I am not of the body,' is it therefore not of the body? If the whole body were an eye, where would be the hearing? If the whole were hearing, where would be the smelling? But now God has set the members, each one of them, in the body just as He pleased. And if they were all one member, where would the body be? But now indeed there are many members, yet one body. And the eye cannot say to the hand, 'I have no need of you'; nor again the head to the feet, 'I have no need of you.' No, much rather, those members of the body which seem to be weaker are necessary. And those members of the body which we think to be less honorable, on these we bestow greater honor; and our unpresentable parts have greater modesty, but our presentable parts have no need. But God composed the body, having given greater honor to that part which lacks it, that there should be no schism in the body, but that the members should have the same care for one another. And if one member suffers, all the members suffer with it; or if one member is honored, all the members rejoice with it. Now you are the body of Christ, and members individually. And God has appointed these in the church: first apostles, second prophets, third teachers, after that miracles, then gifts of healings, helps, administrations, varieties of tongues. Are all apostles? Are all prophets? Are all teachers? Are all workers of miracles? Do all have gifts of healings? Do all speak with tongues? Do all interpret?

But earnestly desire the best gifts. And yet I show you a more excellent way."

1 Corinthians 14:1, 12 (NKJ) "Pursue love, and desire spiritual gifts, but especially that you may prophesy....Even so you, since you are zealous for spiritual gifts, let it be for the edification of the church that you seek to excel." and

Ephesians 4:8-12 (NKJ) "Therefore He says: 'When He ascended on high, he led captivity captive, and gave gifts to men' ... And He Himself gave some to be apostles, some prophets, some evangelists, and some pastors and teachers, for the equipping of the saints for the work of ministry, for the edifying of the body of Christ,"

Do remember that God has made you consistent with His plan for your life and therefore, you will find an easier fit with your skills, abilities and aptitude for the ministry designed for you.

5.10   How to meditate? *

First we must realize that meditation requires an ***object to meditate*** upon. The Biblical objects are at least seven-fold and include *the book of the law, the law of the Lord, the Lord himself, His works, His word, His statues*, and *His precepts*. The following scriptures illustrate this:

Joshua 1:8 (KJV) "This **book of the law** shall not depart out of thy mouth; but thou shalt meditate therein day and night, that thou mayest observe to do according to all that is written therein: for then thou shalt make thy way prosperous, and then thou shalt have good success."

Psalms 1:2 (KJV) "But his delight is in the **law of the LORD**; and in his law doth he meditate day and night."

Psalms 63:6 (KJV) "When I remember thee upon my bed, and meditate on **thee** in the night watches."

Psalms 77:12 (KJV) "I will meditate also of all **thy work**, and talk of thy doings."

Psalms 119:15 (KJV) "I will meditate in **thy precepts**, and have respect unto thy ways."

Psalms 119:23 (KJV) "Princes also did sit and speak against me: but thy servant did meditate in **thy statutes**."

Psalms 119:48 (KJV) "My hands also will I lift up unto thy commandments, which I have loved; and I will meditate in **thy statutes**."

Psalms 119:78 (KJV) "Let the proud be ashamed; for they dealt perversely with me without a cause: but I will meditate in **thy precepts**."

Psalms 119:148 (KJV) "Mine eyes prevent the night watches, that I might meditate in **thy word**." and

Psalms 143:5 (KJV) "I remember the days of old; I meditate on all **thy works**; I muse on the work of thy hands."

<u>One could also practice **Divine Reading**</u> as outlined by Pastor Hal Harter [12] in the following:

DIVINE READING

My Approach.

1. Be quiet before the LORD. KNOW that you are in the Presence of the LORD. Relax. GOD loves you as you are.

2. Write on a piece of paper a SCRIPTURE passage or a verse.

3. Then just sit quietly in the Presence of GOD.

4. Don't think about the SCRIPTURE. Just be quiet before HIM.

5. If any thoughts come to mind, write them down. It doesn't matter what they might sound like, just write them down.

6. Then check them against SCRIPTURE.

7. THANK GOD FOR HIS PERSONAL WORD TO YOU.

8. Then do it.

(Ask the LORD any question you desire an answer to and follow this procedure.)

(REMEMBER THIS IS HEART TO HEART, SPIRIT TO SPIRIT - NOT MIND TO MIND OR FEELING TO FEELING.)

<u>But what about meditating upon or within ourselves?</u> **The basic problem is that there is nothing good in us**! We see this **WARNING** in the following Scriptures:

Psalms 36:1-4 (KJV) "The transgression of the wicked saith within my heart, that there is no fear of God before his eyes. For he flattereth himself in his own eyes, until his iniquity be found to be hateful. The words of his mouth are iniquity and deceit: he hath left off to be wise, and to do good. He **deviseth mischief upon his bed**; he setteth himself in a way that is not good; he abhorreth not evil."

Romans 3:9-12 (KJV) "What then? are we better than they? No, in no wise: for we have before proved both Jews and Gentiles, that they are all under sin; As it is written, **There is none righteous, no, not one**: There is none that understandeth, there is none that seeketh after God. They are all gone out of the way, they are together become unprofitable; there is none that doeth good, no, not one."

Romans 7:18-19 (KJV) "For I know that in me (that is, in my flesh,) dwelleth no good thing: for to will is present with me; but how to perform that which is good I find not. For the good that I would I do not: but the evil which I would not, that I do."

But what about meditating upon meditation itself? This is only meditation upon a concept or abstract idea and utilizes **rhythmic breathing.** According to Schroeder [13] "Perhaps it is because controlling our breathing touches such a deep part of the brain that conscious deep inhaling and exhaling is such a relaxing exercise." However, this exercise has a **GREAT DANGER** and it is that the brain is 'a machine that a ghost can operate' [14] when disengaged from logic and reason. This occurs during periods of meditation because the information gathered during these periods goes directly into the subconscious, helping to set up the pre-suppositions upon which the framework of life is based. The preceding process by-passes our own logic-and-reason rules (See [15]).

CHAPTER 6 – BAPTISM

6.1   What is the difference in being baptized in water and in the Holy Spirit, and [what is] the importance of both? Or what is the necessity for Two Baptisms?

There are <u>*actually three levels*</u> of baptism written about in [16]. In the first, "The Holy Spirit is the baptizer, the church is the element into which he baptizes, and the unregenerated sinner is the object that is baptized". In the second, "The Church is the agent, water is the element and the new Christian is the object"; and in the third, "The regenerated sinner, now a member of the Christian Church, must be baptized in the Holy Spirit by the Lord Jesus Christ, the head of the Church. Christ is the agent, the Holy Spirit is the element, and the believer is the object."

When I learned of these three baptisms, I wondered *how exactly* Jesus did the last one when the scriptures teach that the Father is involved. Then it became clear to me that His role is to **<u>pray</u>** the Father when the believer has loved Jesus and followed His commandments. This can be seen clearly by a study of **Matthew 3:11**, **John 14:15-16, 26,** and **Luke 11:13**. In particular, we learn from:

Matthew 3:11 (KJV) "I indeed baptize you with water unto repentance: but he that cometh after me is mightier than I, whose shoes I am not worthy to bear: he shall baptize you with the Holy Ghost, and with fire" and from

John 14:15-16 (KJV) that "If ye love me, keep my commandments. And I will pray the Father, and he shall give you another Comforter, that he may abide with you for ever;" and from

John 14:26 (KJV) "But the Comforter, which is the Holy Ghost, whom the Father will send in my name, he shall teach you all things, and bring all things to your remembrance, whatsoever I have said unto you." and from

Luke 11:13 (KJV) "If ye then, being evil, know how to give good gifts unto your children: how much more shall your heavenly Father give the Holy Spirit to them that ask him?"

Regarding the baptism in water, [17] reports that it comes "from the Greek word 'baptizo (bap-tid'-zo); from a derivative of *Strong's Word 911*; to immerse, submerge; to make overwhelmed (i.e. fully wet); used only (in the N. T.) of ceremonial ablution, especially (technically) of the ordinance of Christian baptism: KJV– Baptist, baptize, wash."

Romans 6:4 (KJV) conveys this idea with "Therefore we are buried with him by baptism into death: that like as Christ was raised up from the dead by the glory of the Father, even so we also should walk in newness of life." and

Colossians 2:12-14 (KJV) "Buried with him in baptism, wherein also ye are risen with him through the faith of the operation of God, who hath raised him from the dead. And you, being dead in your sins and the uncircumcision of your flesh, hath he quickened together with him, having forgiven you all trespasses; Blotting out the handwriting of ordinances that was against us, which was contrary to us, and took it out of the way, nailing it to his cross;" conveys the same idea.

6.2 *Should we get baptized again as an adult, or is one time sufficient?*

6.3 *Should I get baptized more than once?*

6.4 *How many times are you supposed to be baptized?*

My answer to the above three questions is basically this: once should be enough when you have done so with the right (mature) understanding and attitude. However, as we go though life, if there has been a falling away (backsliding) followed by repentance or a significant increase in devotion to Jesus, marked with new beginnings, and we wish to signify either of these events with a new commitment, re-baptism would be appropriate.

CHAPTER 7 – SPEAKING IN TONGUES

7.1 *What is 'speaking in tongues'? What does it mean and should we use it?* *

All speaking *is in tongues*; however, there are four kinds of tongues referred to in **1 Corinthians 13:1** and in **1 Corinthian 14**. The tongues of men are <u>two-fold</u>: namely, a language known to the believer *or* a known language among men but unknown to the speaker. The other tongues, sometimes called angel speech or heavenly language, are also <u>two-fold</u>: namely, a prayer language unknown to the believer and to other people *or* Holy Spirit-inspired speech in a congregation that is to be followed by an interpretation with a result equivalent to prophecy. We learn from **1 Corinthians 14:2** that the man/person who speaks in an unknown tongue edifies himself in the things of God, and we all need that.

7.2 *Is 'speaking in tongues' scriptural for today's believer?*

7.3 *What about speaking in tongues in church for everyone?*

Some people will use **1 Corinthians 13:8** as an indication that 'tongues' or glossolalia (one naturally <u>*unacquired*</u> [17], heavenly language or angel speech) will cease, but this same passage says that knowledge will vanish away. We use knowledge today, so if that has not vanished, neither should the church forbid speaking in tongues. Moreover, **1 Corinthians 14:39-40 (NKJ)** reports that "Therefore, brethren, desire earnestly to prophesy, and do not forbid to speak with tongues. Let all things be done decently and in order." So, in a church service there is a caution, reinforced by **1 Corinthians 14:26-28**, but not in a believer's private life.

7.4 Day of Pentecost – speaking in tongues – What this all about?

This was the initial outpouring of the Holy Spirit upon those gathered in the Upper Room who had waited there, as Jesus commanded, until they received the "promise made by my Father…" (**Acts 1:4-5 NEB**). The words spoken by those leaving the Upper Room ***glorified God in the native language*** (**Acts 2:6-11 NEB**) of those Jews who were from various parts of the world and had come to Jerusalem for the Feast of Pentecost. Moreover, it produced the affect of getting people's attention, so that Peter could stand up and preach a sermon to them about Jesus and their need for salvation through His name. (**Acts 2:14-41 NEB**)

7.5 If you have the Holy Spirit, is the only way to know it if you speak in tongues?

Some church denominations teach that this is true, including my own. However, my personal experience is that you can be filled with the Holy Spirit without the release in your prayer language. It was so in my case. After being prayed for many times by various people without receiving a prayer language, I said to God; either you are a liar or I have been filled, because I had done what was required by Scripture. Since I knew God <u>not</u> to be a liar, I asked my spirit man if the Holy Spirit had come, and He said 'YES'! This was reassuring, but I still needed a release in the language. It happened a few months later after a prayer meeting.

Chapter 8 – Other Topics

8.1 *How to Fast?*

Let us consider the *purpose, method*, what is *accomplished*, and some *practical* considerations of fasting.

Firstly, the real *purpose* of a fast is to build up the spirit man by helping him to focus on the things of God. Consider, as a guide,

Isaiah 58:6-11 (NKJ) which says "Is this not the fast that I have chosen: to loose the bonds of wickedness, to undo the heavy burdens, to let the oppressed go free, and that you break every yoke? Is it not to share your bread with the hungry, and that you bring to your house the poor who are cast out; when you see the naked, that you cover him, and not hide yourself from your own flesh? Then your light shall break forth like the morning, your healing shall spring forth speedily, and your righteousness shall go before you; the glory of the LORD shall be your rear guard. Then you shall call, and the LORD will answer; you shall cry, and He will say, 'Here I am.' If you take away the yoke from your midst, the pointing of the finger, and speaking wickedness, If you extend your soul to the hungry and satisfy the afflicted soul, then your light shall dawn in the darkness, and your darkness shall be as the noonday. The LORD will guide you continually, and satisfy your soul in drought, and strengthen your bones; you shall be like a watered garden, and like a spring of water, whose waters do not fail."

Secondly, the *method* is covered in

Matthew 6:16-18 (NKJ) as "Moreover, when you fast, do not be like the hypocrites, with a sad countenance. For they disfigure their faces that they may appear to men to be fasting.

Assuredly, I say to you, they have their reward. But you, when you fast, anoint your head and wash your face, so that you do not appear to men to be fasting, but to your Father who is in the secret place; and your Father who sees in secret will reward you openly."

Thirdly, what is *accomplished* can be found in gospel account given in

Mark 9:26-29 (KJV) "And the spirit cried, and rent him sore, and came out of him: and he was as one dead; insomuch that many said, He is dead. But Jesus took him by the hand, and lifted him up; and he arose. And when he was come into the house, his disciples asked him privately, Why could not we cast him out? And he said unto them, This kind can come forth by nothing, but by prayer and fasting."

Fourthly, there are some *practical* matters to consider that include a variety of fasts. A partial list of fasting types follows: there is the Daniel fast (**Daniel 1:8-16**); there is one which includes the skipping of meals but drinking only water and juice; and there will be some people, due to medical conditions, who are unable to fast food, but they can fast other things that compete for the attention of God. Note that after two-three days, many find that the hunger pains will subside.

8.2   Was Jesus a short man?

If we look at four different Scriptural translations of **Luke 19:1-3**, we find that:

KJV "And Jesus entered and passed through Jericho. And, behold, there was a man named Zacchaeus, which was the chief among the publicans, and he was rich. And he sought to see Jesus who he was; and could not for the press, because he was little of stature."

NAS "And He entered and was passing through Jericho. And behold, there was a man called by the name of Zaccheus; and he was a chief tax-gatherer, and he was rich. And he was trying to see who Jesus was, and he was unable because of the crowd, for he was small in stature."

NIV "Jesus entered Jericho and was passing through. A man was there by the name of Zacchaeus; he was a chief tax collector and was wealthy. He wanted to see who Jesus was, *but being a short man he could not*, because of the crowd."

NKJV "Then Jesus entered and passed through Jericho. Now behold, there was a man named Zacchaeus who was a chief tax collector, and he was rich. And he sought to see who Jesus was, but could not because of the crowd, for he was of short stature."

Based on the preceding four renderings of this account, there are only three possibilities: 1-Jesus was short, 2-Zacchaeus was short or 3-they were both short. If Jesus was short, it would have been difficult for Zacchaeus to see him with the crowd in the way. But, as this is the only account where the height or stature of Jesus **is possibly mentioned**, if Jesus were a short man, it should have shown up in other accounts of His ministry. For example, people with distinguishing features, such as great height/stature, are specifically mentioned in the Old Testament – See **2 Samuel 21:20; 1 Chronicles 11:23**; & **1 Chronicles 20:6**. Therefore, the person being referred to as being of short stature <u>must be</u> Zacchaeus.

8.3 Why is there so much jealousy in the human race?

Scripture answers this in

Galatians 5:19-23 (KJV) "Now the works of the flesh are manifest, which are these; Adultery, fornication,

uncleanness, lasciviousness, idolatry, witchcraft, hatred, variance, emulations, wrath, strife, seditions, heresies, *envyings*, murders, drunkenness, revellings, and such like: of the which I tell you before, as I have also told you in time past, that they which do such things shall not inherit the kingdom of God. **But** the fruit of the Spirit is love, joy, peace, longsuffering, gentleness, goodness, faith, Meekness, temperance: against such there is no law."

Therefore, the basic answer is that the human race operates in the realm of the flesh rather than that of the spirit.

8.4 Did it rain before Noah's ark? Or when did rain begin?

In **Genesis 2:5-6 (KJV)** it is recorded that "And every plant of the field before it was in the earth, and every herb of the field before it grew: for the LORD God had not caused it to rain upon the earth, and there was not a man to till the ground. **But there went up a mist from the earth, and watered the whole face of the ground**." And in

Genesis 7:4 (KJV) it is recorded that "For yet seven days, and I will cause it to rain upon the earth forty days and forty nights; and every living substance that I have made will I destroy from off the face of the earth."

Therefore, according to Scripture, there was no rain before Noah's time; it commenced to rain only after the ark was completed with Noah's family and the animals aboard.

CHAPTER 9 – CLOSING THOUGHTS

This book has been written from the viewpoint of the inmates and is a fair representation of the questions that a changing group of men over the years have had at one penal institution. The questions may or may not be new to you, but the fact that the inmates have voiced them and are sincerely interested in having answers to help them in their Christian walk may prove helpful to others engaged in a prison, jail or other ministry. The fundamental premise of this book is that any group of thinking adults will have questions and, if you want to know how to minister to these people, first ask what questions they have and then try to address them as quickly as possible.

Lastly, I would encourage my brothers/sisters in the Christian community to teach the fundamentals of Christ and the reality of the Holy Spirit (See **Hebrews 6:1-2**, for example) so that the questions being addressed in this book by believers will be answered before they can be asked. This, then, will open up opportunities for a new level of questions in which the pastors/ministers/teachers will be able to seek God for answers and to teach their congregations new truths about Jesus Christ and the mission left for us.

Let us move beyond programs and meetings to experience the Lord Jesus more frequently and in more sustainable ways. This will change the world in which we live.

REFERENCES

[1]. *Nelson's Illustrated Bible Dictionary.* (Copyright © 1986, Thomas Nelson Publishers).

[2]. *International Standard Bible Encylopaedia.* (Electronic Database Copyright © 1996 by Biblesoft).

[3] Nee, Watchman: *The normal Christian Life.* Christian Literature Crusade, Printed in Great Britian by Fletcher & Son Ltd, Norwich, 1967.

[4]. Kennedy, D. James: *What's so Amazing about Grace?* Coral Ridge Ministries, P. O. Box 14216, Ft. Lauderdale, FL 33302-4216, (8IV) 693260.

[5]. M. H. Shakir, translator: *The Qur'an.* Tahrike Tarsile Qur'an, Inc. 80-08 51st Ave., Elmhurst, NY 11373, 2005, pp. 34-35, 337.

[6]. Woodward, Dick: Mini-Bible College: The Whole Word for the Whole World – Old Testament Handbook. International Cooperating Ministries, 1995.

[7]. *Outline from Nave's Topical Bible.* (Electronic Database Copyright © 1996 by Biblesoft).

[8]. Kennedy, D. James: *The Real Meaning of the ZODIAC.* CRM Publishing, 1997.

[9]. Larson, Rick: *The Star of Bethlehem.* Mpower Pictures and Stephen Vidano Films, 2009.

[10]. Beach, Charles R.; and Albert, Leonard C.: *Men's Fellowship Lay Coordinator's Manual.* Pathway Press, Cleveland, TN, 1980, p. 252.

[11]. Ortiz, Juan Carlos: *Living with Jesus Today.* Creation House, Carol Stream, IL, 1982,

[12]. Harter, Pastor Hal: *Divine Reading.* Self Published, August 17, 2003.

[13]. Schroeder, Gerald, L.: *The Hidden Face of God: How Science Reveals the Ultimate Truth.* A Touchstone Book/Published by Simon & Schuster, New York, 2001, p. 131.

[14]. *Gods of the New Age.* Jeremiah Films, VHS 13003, 1988.

[15]. Klein, Ken: Cracking the Code: The Beast of the Earth Rises (DVD). Ken Klein Productions, 2001.

[16]. Du Plessis, David J.: *The Spirit Bade Me Go.* Logos International, 1970, pp.70, 77.

[17]. Strong, James: *Strong's Greek/Hebrew Dictionary.* (The Exhaustive Concordance of The Bible), Abingdon Nashville, ©, 1890 by James Strong, Madison, NJ.

[18]. Schenck, Paul; with Schenck, Robert L.: *The Extermination of Christianity – A Tyranny of Consensus.* Huntington House Publishers, 1993, p. 175.

APPENDIX

This appendix covers topics related to the questions posed but are not a part of the direct answer. These topics are, therefore, considered important but supplemental material for the reader.

*Related to the **Questions 2.5** – Godhead – Not man-made*

Our (Trinity) God embodies holiness by His **very nature**, unlike what people have followed in the past as recorded in **Galatians 4:8 (NKJ)** "But then, indeed, when you did not know God, you served those which by nature are not gods."

Related to **Question 2.11** – Events in the Book of Revelation

We need to understand that the Book of Revelation is just the final summing up of what is already at work in this world. Consider the following Scriptures:

Ephesians 2:1-2 (NIV) "As for you, you were dead in your transgressions and sins, in which you used to live when you followed the ways of this world and **of the ruler of the kingdom of the air**, the spirit who is now at work in those who are disobedient." And **I John 5:19 (NIV)** "We know that we are children of God, and *that the whole world is under the control of the evil one.*"

The power of darkness is NOW increasing and encroaching in every aspect of life that it can. Christians will come under increasing attack, little by little, as the world system – ***THE BEAST*** [15] – tries to strip us of our 'rights'. As in Nazi Germany, "The first step in the progression toward persecution of persons is identification. The second is marginalization; the third, vilification; the fourth, criminalization; and, finally, persecution. [18]"

Related to **Questions 4.1 & 2.31** – Heaven & Faith

Different religious groups have different understandings of heaven. For:

Christians and Messianic Jews – A sinless place where God dwells and is offered to those who have had their sins removed by repentance and application of the shed blood of Jesus/Yeshua, the Messiah, to their lives. Jesus said that in heaven men do not marry and are not given in marriage, but are like the angels – eunuchs. We find this in **Matthew 22:30 (NIV)** "At the resurrection people will neither marry nor be given in marriage; they will be like the angels in heaven." – NO SEX!!

As an aside, some Christian denominations, and certainly all cultic groups, teach that you have to be in their church or group and be initiated or baptized into their ways to enter heaven. This 'my-way or the highway attitude' has got to be a problem for the average person who is trying to live a Christian life. The Bible only teaches that you have to be ***born-again and know Jesus*** in order to enter into the Kingdom of God, no matter in which Christian denomination you choose to fellowship or worship. Those groups which claim exclusivity to God and His Kingdom need to recheck the Bible.

Jews – For those whose names are still in 'The Book of Life'. Also, "Heaven is where the soul experiences the greatest possible pleasure - the feeling of closeness to G-d. Of course not all souls experience that to the same degree. It's like going to a symphony concert. Some tickets are front-row center; others are back in the bleachers. Where your seat is located is based on the merit of your good deeds - e.g. giving charity, caring for others, prayer.

A second factor in heaven is your understanding of the environment. Just like at the concert, a person can have great seats but no appreciation of what's going on. If a person spends their lifetime elevating the soul and becoming sensitive to spiritual realities (through Torah study), then that will translate into unimaginable pleasure in heaven. On the other hand, if life was all about pizza and football, well, that can get pretty boring for eternity."

judaism.about.com/library/3_askrabbi_o/bl_simmons_heaven hell.htm

Moslems – Where Allah lives and where the Moslem earns his way in by obeying the five tenets. Depending on how he lives/dies here, he may receive 72 virgins for endless sex.

Mormons – They have three heavens.

http://en.wikipedia.org/wiki/File:The_Plan_of_Salvation.jpg

At the Final Judgment the judges, *Elohim, Jesus, and Joseph Smith*, decide who goes where. The Mormon man and wife couples chosen to go to the Celestial Kingdom (highest heaven) have endless sex resulting in an endless supply of spiritual babies to be put into human bodies on some planet.

Buddhists – Nirvana- paradise, bliss or ecstasy. No more problems.

Hindus – Final reincarnation in which nothing more prevents the person from entering into it. Can also be classified as achieving Godhood!

So who is right? –

Is there more than one heaven?

Does each religion have a separate place to go?

Suppose only one of these groups is correct, what happens to those who believe differently?

I endorse the one for which there is evidence of life after death, as reported in those who have been resuscitated and detailed the events which happened to them. This is the Christian belief.

*Related to **Question 5.10** – Who we are*

We need to be in the group that are "becomers" rather than "be'ers". A "becomer" is one who has not yet arrived but knows that he/she is in Christ Jesus; whereas, the "be'er" is someone who is satisfied with just being himself/herself, and that typically outside of Christ.

Related to **Question 7.1** – Heavenly language [16]

"A Serious Confession[16]

Ministers, missionaries, and others have come to me and said something like this: 'I received the baptism in the Holy Spirit long ago. At the time I spoke in tongues just a little, a sign [**I Corinthians 1:22**] but never again after that. Now I have no further manifestations of the Spirit. I fear that my ministry is cold, even though I claim the baptism in the Spirit. I do not know that overflowing fullness that I believe I should have. Is it because I have not continued to pray with tongues?'

Candidly, I believe it is. You have missed the secret of praying and worshipping in the Spirit. You have prayed 'with the understanding' and your intellect has been very active, but your spirit has been starved because you have failed to pray 'with the sprit.' ...

'Is it not generally accepted that tongues are the least of all the gifts of the Spirit?' Yes, that may be so. But that is the very reason why you should begin with this manifestation, and the others will follow. Praying with unknown tongues will so edify you that you will soon be able to edify the Church. He first edifies you, then the church through you."

www.ingramcontent.com/pod-product-compliance
Lightning Source LLC
LaVergne TN
LVHW051956060526
838201LV00059B/3679